What in the World Are You Doing?

By Cheryl "Action" Jackson

What in the World Are You Doing?

Copyright © 2011 by Cheryl Jackson

Published in the United States by
INSIGHT PUBLISHING
Sevierville, Tennessee • www.insightpublishing.com
ISBN 978-1-60013-600-9
Cover Design: Greg Lakloufi
Interior Format and Design: Chris Ott

Dedicated to my husband, Artis and my adorable sons,
Robert and Artis Jr., for your patience, love and support.
To my parents, Robert Hawthorne and Minnie Hawthorne-Ewing,
who prayed for me, without ceasing.

Table of Contents

Acknowledgments

You and I were born for a purpose. When you are following the plan that God has designed for your life, your purpose is revealed and your dreams come true. For years, people have told me to put my stories in writing. But it was Mr. Zig Ziglar who finally commanded, "Stop speaking and start writing! There is nothing like the joy that comes when you encourage somebody, and I believe you can write a best seller!" Thanks to Mr. Ziglar, I was finally motivated to birth this book and inspire others to succeed. I found a writer, Karin Velez, an editor, Amy Zinger, and a friend, Greg Lakloufi who graciously helped me put my voice on paper. To them, I am grateful. I'm also forever indebted to Laurie Magers.

To Ms. Oprah Winfrey, thank you for being an inspiration to so many. I want you to know what just one kind word, one sentence — "Yes, I will grant you an interview" — did to a plain ol' girl from Dallas, Texas.

To Saint Elizabeth Ann Seton, and especially to Father Henry, Tony Fleo, Joyce Neal, Denny and Jewel Beran, Bill and Kasey Hollen, Diane Geracie and the entire congregation who continue to deliver finances, countless volunteer hours and food to Minnie's Food Pantry, thank you. A deep and heartfelt thanks to Trilanda Lewis, who spent countless hours and many sleepless nights helping me bring The Giving Movement organization to life. To Wal-Mart Corporation, Nikki Bayne, Stephen Paige, Kevin Crawford, and Coleman Taylor for helping me "Feed Just One." Thanks to Market Street Corporation and Robert, the manager in Plano, Texas, for donating to Minnie's Food Pantry. You should see the smiles when I give a hungry person a steak, fresh salad and fruit from your store. It is priceless.

This book is as much about my family as it is about me, and I am blessed beyond words to have my husband, Artis Jackson, who can recount every crazy thing that I have done or dreamed, but somehow continues to love me. I love and adore you. To my beautiful sons, R.J. and Artis, Jr., I give thanks, ask for forgiveness and promise to become the mother and friend you need me to be. I am so proud of you both.

To my brothers, Robert, Gerald, Tony, Eric, and Darius, and to my baby sister, Lynette, I celebrate our bond and history. Thank you to my best friend, Erica Simon, for believing in my dream, in spite of what your eyes saw. We walked by faith. To Christie and Danielle, thank you for being amazing friends and partners in crime (those were the days!). Thank you, Aunt Lil and Aunt Faye, for always being there and telling me not to stop. To DayStar Deliverance Ministries — it took a village to raise me.

To my mother, Minnie Hawthorne' Ewing, you understood the girl I was and you celebrate the woman I am. You were the spirit that guided me until I could hear and understand the voice of God on my own.
To my father, Robert Charles Hawthorne, what a noble man you were. I remember you. I honor you. I will see you again. R.I.P.

And to you, the reader, thank you for feeding the hungry. A portion of the proceeds from each book sold benefits Minnie's Food Pantry. My prayer for you is that you learn to recognize every opportunity as something that happened because you spoke it, God heard it, and He honored your faith.

With gratitude I thank my friends and family wherever you are for supporting and praying for me.

"We make a living but what we get: We make a life by what we give."
- Winston Churchill

Introduction: It's a Wonderful Life

"Strange, isn't it? Each man's life touches so many other lives. When he isn't around, he leaves an awful hole, doesn't he?"
– Clarence the Angel, "It's a Wonderful Life."

It was Christmas Eve, 2009. And as I stood in the snow and sleet, overwhelmed by the wreckage of Minnie's Food Pantry, I couldn't do anything but cry.

Dallas was in the middle of a winter storm that had been pouring buckets of rain and snow all over the city. We hadn't realized that water and snow from the storm had been accumulating on the roof of the warehouse — enough weight to cause a section of the roof to collapse. Water poured in, ceiling tiles crashed to the floor, and months' worth of donations were ruined.

Any boxed goods that got wet had to be discarded. Canned goods had gotten so soaked, the labels had come off, rendering them unfit for distribution. I threw away at least 300 boxes of cereal, shelves of canned and boxed goods, and boxes of produce. I also found that three of our computers had been destroyed. We filled up five dumpsters with thousands of pounds of destroyed food.

I have always been a strong believer that everything happens for a reason. But I just couldn't see a reason for this. I had prayed to God to give me a place to start a food pantry, had prayed to Him to provide for the hungry. So how was it fair that an "act of God" was responsible for the destruction that day? I just couldn't wrap my head around what purpose He would have for allowing this devastation when so many people needed us.

There were many more families that year that had needed food for the Christmas season and to take them into the New Year. The need always seems to be greatest around the holidays, and this year was no exception — only the economy had increased the need tenfold. The previous year, Minnie's Food Pantry had supplied food to around 100 families per month, on average. By the end of 2009 we were providing food for over 1000 families per month. That's a lot of need, a lot of food, and a lot of donations.

Now we would have to reduce the amount of food we could give each family at the start of the year. I couldn't stand the thought of any child going to bed hungry, but as I looked at those dumpsters full of ruined donations, I believed we wouldn't have a choice.

Then I realized we couldn't just sit there and feel bad about what had happened. We had to do something to fix it. It was Christmas Eve; surely the spirit of giving would be at its strongest. I called the local television stations to tell them what had happened. Several stations sent out their crews to do live coverage at Minnie's, and I cried all the way through the interviews. The story aired on three news stations that night, and the anchors asked anyone who could help to call or stop by the pantry. The response was overwhelming.

We had dozens of people and churches rushing in to donate money and food items. And as the door opened and closed with people coming to donate, folks would comment that it seemed like the classic movie, *It's a Wonderful Life*. Until that day, I hadn't seen the movie. It's about a man named George Bailey, portrayed by Jimmy Stewart, who wanted to follow his dreams, but ends up being stuck in his small town running the family savings and loan. At the start of the depression, when there's a run on the banks, he feels as if his life is falling apart.

On Christmas Eve, he decides the world would be better off if he had never been born. As I watched the movie, I identified with every emotion

George was having. Everything that night had seemed hopeless for me. My entire team had worked hundreds of hours to get to this point, only to be surrounded by water, snow and pounds of damaged food.

For George Bailey, a guardian angel named Clarence helped him change his way of thinking. For me, it was a man named George Rosado, who arrived with his 15-year-old son, Carter. He walked in the pantry and said " My wife Mary saw you on the news crying and she said you have to go help her." For hours, they helped throw away spoiled food and cleared buckets of water off the floor. Before he left, George donated $1,000 to help us even further. He also came back a couple days later to donate a space heater. I will never forget him.

My team of volunteers worked nonstop over the holidays, and within four days, we had received almost $4,000 to help replace the food we had lost. We still needed to replace the shelves and computers, but people were still donating food, and I was thankful that we would have something to give at the start of the year. A few days later, a man named Moses came to the pantry and donated $10,000. Does the names Mary and Moses sound familiar to you? God had sent them to me.

The lesson of *It's A Wonderful Life* is simple: we all have our role to play in the world, and we are all important. George Bailey consistently sacrifices things in his life to make sure others can have a better one. For me, the outpouring of the entire community validated that what I was doing was my purpose on this earth. We have to stick together, and that was clear to me as people began to pour into the pantry.

God had known what He was doing. There was a purpose to the destruction. I received phone calls from people who told me they hadn't even known the food pantry existed. Basically, those who wanted to help came, and those who needed help had discovered Minnie's Food Pantry. It reaffirmed my belief that everything happens for a reason, and that there is a plan for our lives. If you are truly doing what you are called to do, nothing can stop you.

This book isn't about me. It's the story of the "angels among us" who have touched me, inspired me, and helped me along this strange and beautiful journey called life. It's the story of those who have taught me that, while you do have to ask for what you want and that persistence does pay, giving to others is the only form of receiving.

You Have Not Because You Ask Not

Ask, and it shall be given you; seek, and you shall find; knock, and it shall be opened unto you. For every one that asks receives; and he that seeks finds; and to him that knocks it shall be opened. – Matthew 7:7-8

I was born in South Dallas, which was the focus of bitter court battles in the early 1970s over the desegregation of schools. I was too young to notice what was happening, but my neighborhood was part of what was called "white flight" during desegregation attempts. Minority families would move to areas they perceived as superior to theirs, and Caucasian middle-class families moved away from urban communities they saw as worsening, which were usually the neighborhoods the minority families were moving into. What was left of the neighborhood in the midst of all this movement was a mostly minority area, known for its poverty and illegal activity. Even today, almost a quarter of the population in that neighborhood is well below the poverty line.

We lived on a street called Prosperity, where, ironically enough, prostitutes plied their trade on every corner. There were just as many vacant, rundown homes and drug houses as there were inhabited ones. Living in a poverty-stricken area could be seen by some as one of the first challenges in my life, but when you're in the situation, you really don't know anything different. There was so much love to go around in our family that we didn't realize we were missing anything.

The first blessing I received in life was my parents. My father, Robert Hawthorne, was born August 13, 1945. He had served as a U.S. Marine, was awarded the National Defense Service Medal, and had been honorably discharged. He married my mom in 1969, helped raised nine children, supported our family and the community, and still went on to get his Masters Degree in Theology. He was an active pastor starting in 1973 and eventually founded DayStar Deliverance Ministries with my mother. He was a true success. My mother, Minnie Bookman, was born December 30, 1945. After getting married, she supported my father in ministry, while raising us kids and devoting much of her time to helping the community. She shined in her role as a pastor's wife, eventually becoming a minister in the church. She was a true giver of time, knowledge, wisdom, and finances. She gave whatever was asked from her and never thought twice. My parents valued their marriage, worked to stay in love, and still had plenty of energy and love left over to give to others.

Mom and Dad worked very hard to give their kids a happy childhood with only age-appropriate concerns and responsibilities. I was aware that we didn't have much money, but they were still able to provide us with happy memories. Every week, we would sit down as a family and play the game, Aggravation. And, boy was it aggravating! The family rule was that we had to play until Dad won. It didn't matter if it took until two o'clock in the morning — if Dad hadn't won, he'd put the coffee on and we'd keep playing. We did everything we could to let him win, but Aggravation doesn't work like that. It's a game of rolling dice and moving marbles, and you can't really *let* anyone win. So we'd play and play until Dad won, and then we'd finally get to go to bed exhausted. But in spite of the ridiculousness of Dad's rule, we had loads of laughs. In addition to that, every Tuesday was family night. From time to time, Mom and Dad would surprise us with a special treat: they would pack all nine of us into our gray station wagon and take us to Showbiz Pizza (which is now called Chuck E. Cheese), where "a kid could be a kid." The rule was that Mom got to play Ms. Pac-Man first. She would play until she had set a high enough score, and then the rest of us kids could play. We had very little money — usually just $2.00 per kid — but we always got to play a few games, and we got to play on the free equipment as much as we wanted.

I recognize that not everyone, regardless of ethnic or socioeconomic group, was as fortunate as we were. I was blessed to have parents who beat the statistical odds. They set the bar very high for their kids, convincing us that we could achieve any goal in life. They taught us that persistence really pays off. If you want something, you have to ask for it. If at first you are told "No," just add a "t" to the end and turn it into "Not yet." Eventually, you'll get what you want. My parents made everything look so effortless that I took it for granted. I hoped to do it just as effortlessly, too, someday.

My father was an amazing man to everyone who knew him, and I wasn't the only one who called him "Papa." He gave the best bear hugs, hugs that instilled confidence in you that you were going to be okay, even when you felt like your world was caving in. He had never met a stranger and had a priceless smile that would light up a room. My father was a lover of life, and giving in every sense of the word. Growing up, he gave me almost anything I wanted. I was his little princess. When he would walk through the door at night, I'd immediately wrap myself around his leg. Of course, if I was the princess, my mom was the queen. My father would drag me across the floor as I held onto his leg, so he could give Mom a kiss first before picking me up.

I idolized my dad. And since he was a plumber by trade before he entered the ministry, I decided that I would be a plumber, too. This announcement must have come as a surprise, but he stifled his smile and took me to work with him when the next opportunity arrived. It just so happened that the next opportunity was a backed-up toilet. I waltzed right in with my tools, and Dad explained to me what we were going to do. After just one look (and a sniff), I immediately changed my mind about becoming a plumber. Dad had known that would be my reaction, but he always gave me opportunities to try something new.

When I was in the fourth grade, my dad gave up plumbing to become a pastor, and we moved 35 miles north to Allen, Texas. Allen is a predominantly white, more affluent suburb of Dallas, and I was definitely in the minority. It was a rough adjustment at such a young age when all I wanted and desired was acceptance. I was already a bit of a perfectionist, and at first, the new school proved to be a challenge as I tried to keep up with the more affluent kids, both academically and socially. My two immediate friends, Phelicia Lee and Kim Mills, helped me make the transition in my new environment.

One change that was more difficult to accept was watching our parents struggle with the never-ending exertion that comes with a life devoted to ministry. In a small church, the only people the congregation has to turn to are the pastor and his wife. In our case, those were our parents. We saw them constantly counseling church members and administering to their pains. We heard the incessant ringing of the phone with calls for assistance or guidance. Our parents gave whatever they had of themselves regardless of what it was — support, clothing, food. If our favorite cereal came in the front door, we never got too excited. More than likely, it would be heading right back out to someone who needed it more than we did. Our house should have had a revolving door. Eventually, my siblings and I became emphatic that we didn't want any part of ministry when we became adults. The sacrifices seemed too great.

After giving up my short-lived dream of following in my father's professional footsteps, I became interested in my mother's line of work. She was an office manager, and got me my first real job when I was thirteen years old. One spring break, she asked if I'd like to fill in for the receptionist at her company. Some kids might have said, "No way, I'm on vacation!" But I was excited to work with an icon — my mom — and hungry to make some money. Mother prepared me for my interview with her boss, and told me I would get $50.00 that week to perform my secretarial duties. I smiled and my eyes lit up just at the thought of being paid.

I rode to work with my mother that morning, and for this momentous occasion, we stopped at Grandy's for breakfast. I ordered a steak biscuit and a cinnamon roll to prepare for my big interview, feeling very grown up and on top of the world. We arrived at the office, and Honey, Mom's boss, asked me to come into her office. Honey was a soft-spoken woman. As I sat there answering her questions, I tried to look self-assured, hoping she didn't see how anxious I was. She explained what she expected from me while I filled in for the week. Then she asked, "How much do you expect to get paid this week?" My heart began to race. I could hear Mom telling me I was going to get $50.00, but what was I to do now that I was being asked how much I *expected* to get paid? My parents had always preached, "You have not because you ask not," and the ball was now in my proverbial court, so I said it. I opened my mouth, and with as much confidence as I could gather, I blurted out, "I would like $200.00 for helping you this week." I don't think I can properly describe the look on Honey's face. This successful woman, my mother's boss, squirmed in her seat across from her 13-year-old interviewee. Her face changed two shades in color and then, as I quietly tilted my head to the side waiting for her response, I heard her say, "Well, okay then."

I didn't mention anything to my mother until our ride home. When mom asked how the interview went, I replied, "It was great. I'll get paid $200.00." I thought mother was going to run over the curb. She had to work for this company for a long time to come, and she easily could have been embarrassed that her inexperienced daughter had just brazenly, albeit unknowingly, negotiated a week's salary just fifty dollars shy of the national average for a professional secretary. After she recovered from her initial shock, mom smiled and was proud, because after all, I had done exactly what my parents had taught me. I had spoken what I wanted — and I had received it.

I grew up surrounded by boys: three older brothers, Robert, Gerald, and Tony, and two younger brothers, Eric and Darius, in addition to my younger sister, Lynette, and two cousins. Out of all my siblings, my best friend growing up was my older brother, Gerald. Gerald was my helper, my confidante. He listened to me and laughed with me, and we generally had an all-around good time. We were very close, especially for a brother and sister. But as he got older, he began to hang around his friends more and was home less often — which meant I began to get in trouble more.

I wasn't the neatest child, especially as far as girls go, and there was something about doing the dishes that I just dreaded. I got more spankings than anyone in our house. I even tried to negotiate my way out of spankings by offering my parents money — only two dollars, because that's all I had — and promising that I would not be disobedient again. Unfortunately, they didn't listen, and at least once a month I was the source of family entertainment as I screamed to the top of my lungs while my father patiently waited for me to run around the house, covering my rear end and pointing out to him that my siblings were laughing at me. He would calmly say, "Next time you will complete your chores, won't you?" Looking back, it's funny, but going through it then was no laughing matter. My only saving grace from getting more spankings was Gerald, because he would help me complete my chores when he was home. Needless to say, I wasn't too excited when Gerald's friend, Artis, stepped into the picture.

Artis was a part of our church ministry and started coming around more frequently as he and Gerald got older. His mother and my mother were best friends, and he and Gerald became best friends, too. This was appalling to me — Gerald was *my* best friend, not to mention my cook and maid. Who did this guy think he was? I was jealous and felt like Gerald was being stolen from me. So, in an effort not to lose my best friend to this new guy, I began hanging around with the both of them. Bless their hearts; they never looked at me as the pestering younger sister, although they were four years my senior. We were always together, and now I had added another brother and best friend in Artis.

Our family was raised on strong faith. My father pastored a Pentecostal Holiness church. It was a true hand clapping, foot stomping, tongue speaking, divine healing, "God will provide everything you need," kind of a church. Our upbringing was very strict: modest dress, no popular music, no movie theaters and strict curfews. Girls didn't wear makeup or jewelry, and we never wore pants. As a young lady, I had to ask permission to hang out with my friends, and I certainly wasn't allowed in any social situations where "inappropriate" activities could occur — which meant anything that took place outside of the church. That didn't stop me from finding ways to be sure I was included in all Artis' and Gerald's activities. I had ample opportunity, too, because Artis really struggled his senior year in high school and came over every afternoon to toil through his homework with Gerald. Even though I was only in the eighth grade, I would try to impress him with my smarts by helping him with his work. And Artis was impressed; in fact, I helped him graduate from high school.

All three of us were the greatest of friends. We got in trouble together, got out of trouble together, laughed and carried on together. When Artis and Gerald graduated, I was there. As they got a little older and I worked my way through high school, Artis began to tell Gerald he was going to marry me. Gerald insisted to Artis that wouldn't happen because he was sure I had no interest in him romantically. Even so, Artis maintained that he would eventually marry me.

All through high school, I was on the A and B honor roll and was headed into my senior year. Any time one of us made straight A's the entire six weeks of a school quarter, my mother would reward us with one hundred dollars. Ever the entrepreneur, I asked my mother what she would give me if I made straight A's my entire senior year on my report card. She immediately said, "One thousand dollars," but it was all or nothing. I thought of all the things I could do with that money — and boldly accepted the challenge. Six weeks later, I marched into the house with all A's; in fact, in one class I made an actual 100 percent on my report card. I repeated the feat next quarter, and the next. When the final six weeks ended, I proudly walked through the door with my final set of straight A's. I was a member of the National Honor Society. I was also one of only 12 students chosen for the Gifted Leaders Are Developed (GLAD) program. When I graduated on June 6, 1986, I marched across that stage confident, heavily decorated and extremely smart — or so I thought. But instead of gloating over what I would do with one thousand dollars, you can imagine my parents' surprise when I announced I was madly in love and intended to get married ... to Artis.

Things had been effortless up to that point, just as I thought they should be from watching my parents. I was successful and ready to move on to the next phase of my life. But life was about to show me that you never stop learning, that smarts don't just come from books or from your parents, and success isn't all that effortless. It's your experiences, your interactions with others, your determination to make something better, and what you give that help you learn and make you smart.

On June 6, 1986, I walked down the aisle at my graduation. One month later, at the age of seventeen, I made the very adult decision to get married. In the eyes of the law, I wasn't yet an adult, so my parents would have to consent for me to marry the man of my dreams. I told my parents they could either sign the paperwork allowing me to get married right away, or I'd do it anyway in a few months when I turned eighteen. My parents, of course, knew arguing with me would be futile. They reluctantly agreed, and I walked down the second of two very different aisles within 30 days of each other.

This was not a fairytale wedding. No huge church with lots of flowers and guests. Most of the guests were my high school classmates and relatives. My mother did my floral bouquet, and each stem she placed in the Styrofoam cup brought a tear to her eye. There was no beautiful white dress with a long flowing train. I borrowed my dress from my cousin, Macy, and looking back, not being able to afford my own gown should have been a clue that we weren't ready to get married. There was no huge fancy reception. My father catered the reception himself, which was okay with me since he was an excellent cook. Such a good cook, in fact, that Artis and I didn't even get to eat; the guests had devoured all the food before we had a chance to get to it.

On our wedding night, Artis and I did something we had never been allowed to do before — we went to the movies. We saw *About Last Night* with Rob Lowe and Demi Moore. The movie was a watered-down version of the play *Sexual Perversity in Chicago*. Looking back, our naiveté was another reason, I suppose, we really weren't ready to be married. Nevertheless, I knew this was what I wanted to do, what I was supposed to do.

Blessings In Disguise

After the excitement of the wedding wore off and everything was said and done, though, I thought to myself, "Oh, my God. What in the world have I done?" I was seventeen and married! I had graduated from high school only a month earlier. Regardless of how much we loved each other, I knew Artis and I would have to struggle to make it. We had no money, no savings and nothing but love to our name. In fact, instead of taking the one thousand dollar report card bonus that I was supposed to receive for making straight A's, I asked my mother if we could have the new sofa she had recently purchased to go in our first apartment. She agreed, and I took it and started my new adult life.

Artis worked doing landscaping and maintenance work and, although I had worked odd jobs off and on since thirteen, I didn't really have extensive work experience. I worked at Ford Middle School earning every penny of $3.50 an hour, bringing home a whopping $350 a month. In 1986, that wasn't much, not by a long shot. We could barely even afford our tiny apartment. To keep a roof over our heads, we often had to go without food, and if we ate three meals in a day, we considered ourselves lucky. But even those sacrifices still weren't enough. We found ourselves evicted every few months for not making rent. My friends were always asking, "Cheryl, what's your phone number now?" because our telephone continued to be disconnected. Of course, when we were able to restore the services, we had to be assigned a new number every time. It became a running joke.

But despite our serious struggles, Artis and I were happy. Our love fed us breakfast, lunch and dinner … and even a little dessert. I suppose that "dessert" was what caused me to suddenly start throwing up each morning, noon and night. I was hugging that toilet for dear life so frequently that I finally went to a doctor. The doctor did his test, and told me what we had suspected. "You're pregnant." I was ecstatic. My mother was ecstatic. Artis was ecstatic. And then reality set in.

We were going to be parents. It's one thing to survive on love when it's just the two of you. It's another thing completely to raise a child with no steady job, no money, and no stable place to live. This child of ours was coming into our very volatile little world in just nine short months. What were we going to do? Work in landscaping was sporadic for Artis at best. My job was hardly enough to pay the utilities each month, and often the choice came down to either eating or having electricity. Artis had no health insurance. How in the world were we going to afford the doctor's visits, tests, sonograms, and labor and delivery costs?

The words my father preached every Sunday and the faith ingrained in me when I was growing up would ring in my head throughout my life, especially in times of adversity. They certainly rang loudly now. "God will provide." As the birth of our child drew nearer, we hoped and prayed for just that.

Time after time, medical practices told us they didn't take patients without insurance, but I refused to be one of those mothers who went the entire pregnancy with no prenatal care. I needed to know our baby would be healthy from the beginning, and I wasn't going to let a lack of insurance stand in my way. We looked at midwives, home births, and a slew of different doctors to no avail. When people asked me why I wanted to use a midwife, I would respond by saying I wanted to have a natural childbirth. The truth was that they were cheaper than a regular doctor and I wouldn't have to pay for the hospital. That's what we needed: a cheap place to have a baby.

Weeks went by with no success. Finally, in desperation, I called the best medical practice in the city. I knew it was a long shot, but I had no other options. When I explained our situation, Dr. Raymond offered to let us make periodic payments toward my prenatal care and delivery fees. I cried in relief. God had indeed provided, and our baby would receive the best care modern medicine could provide. This doctor was one in a long line of angels who would step in to help us when we most needed it. When the time came for my sonogram, we were a bundle of nerves. But Dr. Raymond put our minds at ease when he said everything was perfect, and that our baby would enter the world around December 27. Then, it was time for the moment of truth. The doctor grinned and said, "Congratulations. You're having a boy." Artis and I already knew his name: Robert, after my father.

My pregnancy made me sicker than I had ever been in my life. I had developed low blood pressure and anemia, which was causing me to faint. To ensure the baby and I would both stay healthy, I had to take five iron pills a day. This just added another expense to our already Titanic-sized debt. Even with the iron pills, the smell of cooking food made me so violently ill that Artis had to be in charge of preparing all the meals. He was extremely tired from working, but I couldn't cook for him, much less myself. Every night, he came home exhausted, made his own dinner, and cared for me. This should have been an exciting time in our life. We were married, but we found ourselves moving from house to house at the first of every month when rent came due, and although we were expecting our first child, our situation was taking a toll on our relationship. Every time we thought things couldn't get worse, they did.

My faith in "God will provide" was already beginning to falter, but then, when I was seven months pregnant, we lost yet another rental home. Our car became our new home. It felt like complete failure. It *was* complete failure. I didn't understand. My husband had a job. How could we be homeless? The word conjured up images of living in cardboard boxes on the street, dirty and hungry. I thought of people I had encountered in the city, standing with signs asking for help or sitting on the street with their hands outstretched, begging for someone to give them some change. We couldn't let anyone know the situation we were in. Call it pride, determination or stupidity, but we kept everything we owned in our car and stayed nights with friends who were barely scraping by themselves. We were too proud to admit the ugly truth to anyone — not even the friends we were staying with. Even at the lowest point in our lives, we were still luckier than some, and I recognized that. We weren't on the street. And we had the car — a way to get around and a place to keep our possessions.

When I think back on it now, it seems that time in my life lasted much longer than it actually did. It felt like years had passed, but it was just a month before our car — along with all our belongings — was repossessed. We truly had nothing at that point. Nothing but each other and a baby due in a month. It was finally time to swallow our pride and confess the situation to our loved ones — not because we wanted charity, but because we couldn't bear the thought of bringing our child into the world homeless. Artis already blamed himself for everything, and now he had to do what he had most dreaded: admit to my father after just a year and a half of marriage that he couldn't provide for me. But my father was not the kind of man to judge anyone, and he loved Artis like his own son. The only thing my parents were angry about was that we had been too proud to ask for help. And I know now that they were right to be angry.

We moved in with my brother Gerald, which was bad in its own way. He had a tiny apartment in a rough part of town — and didn't even have a lock on his apartment door. We had to use a chair to keep it closed. It got so scary that, when a couple got into a huge fight downstairs and the police came, we finally knew we had to leave. But by the grace of God, we quickly found a new apartment. Not only did we move, but Gerald also moved to the new apartments we'd chosen. That Thanksgiving was the most poignant of our lives, as Artis and I realized losing the car was a blessing in disguise. It was God's way of teaching us that, even though all we had owned was a beaten up car full of clothing, we had still allowed our few possessions to keep us from the full extent of His provision. When we had absolutely nothing, we were overwhelmed with our families' outpouring of love, support, and forgiveness. Artis and I slowly began to get back on our feet — and to prepare for the birth of our son.

That last month just flew by, and before we knew it, we were celebrating Christmas. My father prepared all the fixings for a wonderful dinner. Smoked turkey, roasted chicken and dressing, mustard greens, candied sweet potatoes (which were my favorite), all spread out on the table in glorious abundance. All the best that southern cooking had to offer. My appetite was finally back, and I ate, and I ate, and then I ate some more. My father joked with me, saying, "Cheryl, you're going to eat yourself into labor!" I just laughed and helped myself to another delicious helping of sweet potatoes. Dad just shook his head. "All right, but don't call me at one o'clock in the morning saying you're in labor. I'm not getting up that early."

On December 27, at about one o'clock in the morning, my water broke. When I told Artis, he just looked at me in shock. He seemed paralyzed. He had purchased a special hospital outfit for the occasion but made no move to go get dressed. As he stood there in disbelief I said again, "Honey, it's time. Get ready." Artis finally got dressed — in a completely different outfit than planned — and, still in a daze, called for my brother Gerald, who came running to the rescue.

We slowly loaded ourselves into the car and headed to my parents' house. As my mom squeezed in with us, and my dad took the wheel, he glared at me and said, "I thought I told you not to call me at one o'clock in the morning!" He was joking, of course, because he was just as excited and nervous as we were. So nervous, in fact, that he began to drive the wrong way and we had to turn him around to head to the hospital! As we got closer, the fact that I was in labor was nothing compared to the worries I had about the hospital. At that time, if you showed up at the hospital in labor and you had no insurance, you would be turned away. This fact was in my thoughts the whole way. What would we do if they didn't let us in? Having the baby at home had not been in my plans, but I supposed the doctor would do his job wherever he needed to. Amazingly, though, when we walked into the hospital and the staff realized I was in labor, they took one look at who my doctor was and admitted me immediately, no questions asked. Talk about clout!

I was in labor until 1:07 p.m. on December 27. Twelve hours of excruciating pain, emotional outbursts, crying, laughing and anticipation. At one point, as a contraction swept over me and I cried out in pain, Artis supportively grabbed my hand to help me through it and said, "Aw, c'mon. Take it like a man!" As my face turned purple in rage, my mother intervened. She looked at Artis and said, "Son, I'll be in here with her for a little while. You may want to excuse yourself and take a break." His comment certainly wasn't appreciated at the time, but it makes us laugh now looking back.

After twelve long hours, our 6-pound, 4-ounce, 19-inch son was born healthy and perfect. Robert Jermaine Jackson, named for my father, was instantly the most adorable, precious thing in the world to us.

Life's roller coaster now had us on a wave of highs and lows over this little life we had brought into the world. All at once we were faced with the joys of parenthood and the fears of actual parenting. The magnitude of the situation hit me all at once. I was responsible for a life other than my own. It was my job not only to give R.J. a good home, clean clothes and healthy meals, but also to foster his spirit, his morals and his ambitions. I was responsible for teaching this child, just as my parents had taught me, that every life brought into the world has a purpose. But in reality, I wasn't even quite sure what my own purpose in life was anymore.

The Angels Among Us

You cannot tailor-make the situations in life, but you can tailor-make the attitudes to fit those situations. – Zig Ziglar

I had been so determined at seventeen to be grown up and married. I was to be just like my parents: hard working, strong, in love and successful. But it was beginning to become clear to me that what my parents had made appear so effortless while I was growing up wasn't so effortless after all. I could now look back and see what my parents really had gone through trying to maintain a happy, healthy home environment. As much as Artis and I were in love and loved our son, we were struggling. This whole marriage and family thing wasn't as easy as I thought. I don't know if it was the firm belief in the power of prayer, our belief that "God will provide," or just the odds that in times of desperation something positive is bound to happen, or simply that you have nowhere to go but up. Whatever it was, my mother found an article in the paper that the City of Allen was hiring for a water meter reader. She brought the article to us and, though Artis had no experience in this area, he immediately went to apply. We knew it was a long shot, but had nothing to lose. Unbelievably, Artis got the job and we were over the moon. The job wasn't high paying, but it was steady, provided benefits, and was a big step up for our family.

As we worked to put the pieces of our life back together, we made application after application to find another home to rent. When we were finally approved for a new place to live, we were ecstatic. It felt like a fresh start. We moved into our new home with the few belongings we had, but there was one small problem: we still didn't have a car. That's a bit of a dilemma when it comes to staying employed and taking care of a child. But after the expenses of getting a new place and replacing many of our belongings, there wasn't anything left to buy a vehicle.

Artis' Aunt Esther told us of a car she saw sitting in her neighbor's yard. She didn't think he was doing anything with it and would probably sell it to us if we could manage to give him something for it. Like my parents always taught me, if you want something you have to ask for it. "You have not because you ask not." So, though we barely had a dime to our name, we went to see my aunt's neighbor.

When we walked up to the house, we saw the car in question. It was an old, blue, two-door Cutlass Supreme that had obviously seen better days. But it had four wheels and a motor and presumably ran, so we knocked on the door and introduced ourselves to Mr. Alvin McCrainey. We explained our situation to him and asked if we could somehow buy the car from him. Not only did that wonderful, wonderful man say we could buy the car, but he also said we could make payments to him of just $50 every two weeks. That was it. We were back on track.

If there is one thing I have learned throughout my experiences, it's not to take anything for granted, and we certainly appreciated that car. We were often late on even our small car payments to Mr. McCrainey, so we certainly didn't have any extra money to fix the car if something went wrong. And, believe me; a lot went wrong with that old blue car.

First, the headliner in the car fell out leaving behind a layer of old, nasty, black foam filler. As we would drive, the foam would flake off and fall into my hair, making me look as if I had walked through a storm of black snow.

The air conditioner went out, so we bought a cigarette lighter fan to plug in as our air conditioner. If you've ever lived through a Texas summer you can imagine how little that fan did to cool us off in that car. Then the driver's side window wouldn't roll down so we couldn't even get a breeze to blow through as we drove. Eventually, even the driver's side door refused to open. Imagine pulling up to a drive-thru, rolling down the passenger side window and screaming your order into the speaker from across the other side of the car! Then the battery connections wore out and, in order to start the car, one person would have to pop the hood and hold two wires together while the other turned the ignition. Yep, old blue, Susan was her name, was quite a sight. But she got us from point A to point B, and that was all that mattered. We drove that car into the ground and then kept on driving.

Although Artis worked very hard at his job, his small salary still wasn't enough to make ends meet. I worked odd jobs off and on and found small, albeit brief, success as a speaker and salesperson for a company called Citizens Against Crime. It sounds noble, but in reality, I arranged for community seminars to teach people how to be proactive against crime in their neighborhood and at the end of the seminar would sell them crime deterring items, like pepper spray and glow-in-the-dark "help" signs. I did fine at this job, but unfortunately, the company folded and I had to look for work elsewhere. This was not an easy task. Work was hard to find as it was, and I needed a flexible work schedule to accommodate raising our young son.

At some point, the realization of just how bad off we were really hit home for me. Artis was doing what he could to earn a living. I was trying to raise R.J. and look for work at the same time. This put a large amount of stress on our marriage. It seems that during the times when you should be supporting each other the most and leaning on each other, stress and hardships will cause you and your best friend and partner in life to be at each other's throats. This only serves to make your situation seem more hopeless, and even though your brain is telling you it doesn't make any sense to argue over things you have no control over, your heart and soul says you should have control over everything and should be able to do something about it. I have no idea how my parents made it look so easy all those years. I do know that their strong faith had been passed on to me. At the times I felt the lowest I knew I had to have faith.

One of both our lowest points that year happened when we couldn't even afford diapers. There our young son was, bare-bottomed because we had nothing to put on him and no money to do anything about it. Artis and I even attempted to pin a towel around little R.J.'s bottom to serve as a diaper, arguing about it all the while. I blamed him, he blamed me, and in the meantime little R.J. just smiled as he tinkled on all our sheets. In the midst of this situation there was a knock at the door. It was Artis' Aunt Esther and Uncle John, and they were holding nothing but a package of diapers. How they knew at that moment to bring exactly what we needed is beyond my understanding. Maybe it was part of what my grannies had taught me at such a young age. Giving to others always comes back to you and there's no shame in accepting help. Or what my parent's had taught: "God will provide." Whatever it was, Aunt Esther and Uncle John were our angels that day. It's odd how something as simple as a package of diapers can quell the arguing and fear in a young couple, at least temporarily. We still needed to find a more permanent solution to our worries, but it kept the straw from breaking the camel's back.

I continued to look for work, but one afternoon came home so violently ill I told my husband I needed to go to the hospital. I knew we couldn't afford a doctor's bill but I thought I had pneumonia and knew I needed to be seen right away. Artis patiently listened to me and then calmly said, "You don't have pneumonia. You're just pregnant."

I swear he almost delighted in how angry I got with him. "I am *not* pregnant," I said, and insisted I needed to go to the hospital because I felt like I was about to die. Artis agreed I should go to the hospital if I thought it was necessary, but he would stay home with R.J., who was now nine months old. I was already angry that Artis thought I was pregnant and not sick, and was now infuriated that he wouldn't even accompany me to the hospital while I was so ill. I stormed out, made the nauseous drive to the hospital, explained to the triage nurse what I thought was wrong and was taken in to see the doctor. The doctor ran all kinds of tests and eventually came in to tell me I did, indeed, have pneumonia. I doubt he'd ever seen

24

someone so excited to be so sick. I could now triumphantly march back to my husband and tell him how wrong he was, that I was truly sick and not "just pregnant" as he had so kindly put it, and make him feel bad for not taking me seriously. In reality, I was more excited about not being pregnant than about being right. That was one more stressor I knew I wasn't ready to deal with. Not while we were struggling so much already. The doctor gave me a prescription for medicine for the pneumonia and then, with a thoughtful look that I completely missed at the time, insisted he needed to do just one more test. I didn't even bother to ask him what the test was. When he came back to the room he said, "I need to ask you for that prescription back." I thought for sure that I must have something worse than pneumonia and he needed to prescribe something stronger or, even worse, I needed to be hospitalized. Thank goodness Artis now had benefits through his job. But nothing could have prepared me for the doctor's next words. "Turns out you don't have pneumonia after all," he said. "You're pregnant."

Those words meant something so completely different to me then than the first joyous time I had heard them. My stomach dropped to the floor as I felt my world collapse. How had this happened? Well, I obviously knew *how* it had happened, but why had I *let* it happen? I numbly walked out of the hospital, got in the car and began to cry. And cry. I stopped at my mom's and cried some more. She, on the other hand, was so happy, excited to have another grandbaby on the way. I suppose I should have felt blessed, but I just couldn't share her joy. I knew the financial situation my family was already in. We were hardly able to provide for our first child. What in the world were we going to do now? Artis and my brother Gerald were sitting at the kitchen table when I walked in the door to our home. Artis asked, "Well?" I simply said, "I'm pregnant," walked into our bedroom, closed the door behind me and threw up.

Life was really not working out the way I had planned. Where was the easy success? Why did we have to struggle like this? Why me? Of course, I knew it wouldn't do anyone any good to sit in a self-serving pity party and, once the initial shock wore off, I picked myself back up and became even more determined. I knew I needed to find work; it was even more important now. I figured if I could make enough money each month to at least pay the water bill or the electric bill it would alleviate some of the pressure my poor husband was already feeling trying to support our now growing family.

Unfortunately, this pregnancy had more complications to it than my first. I was even more violently ill than when I was pregnant with R.J., and within the first few months I was diagnosed as being severely anemic. Despite taking five iron pills each day I still suffered from dizziness and lack of energy. Of course, that didn't stop me from looking for a job. The preservation of my family was at stake, after all, and I wasn't going to let something like a little vomiting, dizziness and fatigue stand in my way. I managed to eventually find work as a checkout clerk at a local Winn-Dixie store. The pay was modest at $4.50 per hour, but every little bit helped. It wasn't stimulating work, by any means, and meant hours of standing on my feet each day. I didn't complain at the end of each workday when I came home with sore, swollen feet and felt even more run down as each day passed. Of course, there wasn't any break when I got home because there were chores to do, meals to cook and a child to care for. I was determined to make this work. But I learned determination only goes so far.

During the course of grocery duties one day, I remember checking out customers and watching the items pass one at a time across the scanner. Beep. Beep. I pulled item after item across the little infrared light, listening to the sound of the register adding up the total as each UPC was counted. Beep. Beep. I picked up a bag of dog food and continued my robotic actions while the red light in the scanner seemed to get brighter and the area around my register seemed to get dimmer. Beep. Beep. The next thing I knew, there was no familiar beep, only the eerie feeling of not knowing exactly where I was but that something horrible had just happened. I was nauseous, slightly dizzy and felt like I had been smacked upside the head with a two by four. Then I realized what had happened — I had passed out and fallen face first onto the grocery scanner. The long hours on my feet, combined with my pregnancy-induced anemia, was just too much for my body to handle. I understood then that sheer determination might not be all that I needed to get through the tough times my family was having.

Even though this pregnancy was a struggle, we couldn't help but begin to get excited about the coming of our second child. We decided this time not to find out the gender, but I promised Artis that, if we had a boy, we would name him after his father. Despite our growing excitement, or maybe because of it, the months seemed to drag on. I was no longer able to work, so the burden again fell to Artis. He began to pick up part-time jobs to help make ends meet. He did this all through my pregnancy and finally, our second child, Artis Jr., came into the world just as healthy as could be. He had so much curly hair that my mother shouted "it's a girl" then one final push and Artis Jr. had arrived. His name couldn't have been more perfect. To this day he is just like his father in almost every way. Although he has his father's name, he is still a mama's boy.

We realized, though, that going back to work for me would be futile. Like so many others in our situation, the money I would make would be barely enough to cover daycare for two kids. Artis and I decided we'd rather have our children raised at home than in someone else's care if it wouldn't make a large difference to our financial situation. So we took on the roles my parents had taken on so many years before. I stayed home to raise the children, while my husband worked long hours so we could survive. Our life became such a struggle; we focused so much on work and finances and I became so depressed that poor Artis, Jr. doesn't have nearly as many pictures as his older brother. I probably have only about 10 or 12 baby pictures of Artis, Jr., compared to the hundreds I have of R.J. I still feel guilty about that. If you own a camera, please take the time to photograph the people you love.

As time passed, Artis took on more and more part-time work. Eventually that wonderful man was working four jobs to help us survive. He not only worked his job with the city, but he began working for two different pizza places and delivered newspapers early each morning, seven days a week. I eventually found that I could help Artis a little bit by assisting with the newspaper deliveries, especially on Sundays. Each Saturday night around 11 p.m. we would sit out in front of a store, ironically called Pride, that served as the carrier pickup area, rolling the papers for delivery. We would then go home to get a little bit of rest before heading back out to the pickup point at 2 a.m. to add the advertising circulars to the rolled papers. The only place we could fit the hundreds of papers into our little car was in the trunk. After we loaded the papers and got to the beginning of the route, I would sit in the open trunk of the car as Artis drove slowly down each street yelling back to me, "Left!" or "Right!" I would throw each paper into the appropriate doorstep as he drove. I'm sure we were quite a sight to anyone that happened to be out that early on a Sunday morning.

In general, we were exhausted. My poor husband was working so many hours, he hardly had any time for sleep. I was working just as hard as a wife and mother and assisting him with the newspapers, and I was just plain angry. I was angry at the world, angry with myself, and angry with my husband. I hated the situation we were in. I hated that no matter how hard we worked, we never seemed to get ahead. I hated that life was not working out the way I planned. I hated those early mornings on that paper route so much that sometimes I would hit the front doors as hard as I could when throwing the papers. Sometimes I would intentionally miss the front stoop completely, forcing Artis to have to stop the car to get out and put it where it needed to be, because I was angry. I was just plain fed up with life in general.

For three years, we were on autopilot. Three years of going to work, coming home, doing the chores, feeding the family, going to bed exhausted, and getting up to start it all over again. Pay the bills, rob Peter to pay Paul, rob Paul to pay back Peter, and on and on. Oftentimes we had to decide between food and electricity. Artis would sometimes swing by and drop off pizza orders made by mistake that couldn't be sold, balls of pizza dough leftover at the end of the day, or bags of pepperoni that hadn't been used. Often, that was the only food we had. We finally had to swallow our pride — again — and make the difficult decision to go to the government for help.

I went to the government office and stood in line to be handed a huge stack of paperwork to fill out to request food stamps. It was like writing my life story, only not as fun. The questions were invasive, asking me things like "who can verify your financial situation?" I felt like everyone that walked in knew just why I was there. I was ashamed to ask for this help and felt like I was being judged by the people that worked there, while being treated like just another number. After standing in line to turn in the paperwork and then waiting what seemed like forever for the workers to review it, knowing they contacted the people who could "verify" my situation, I was told we didn't qualify. How could that be? We didn't have money for food or electricity and couldn't feed our kids. How could we not qualify? The worst part about it was the lack of care or understanding in the voices of the workers. They didn't even look at me as I was handed an "emergency" bag of food and sent on my way. I was appreciative to at least have some food, but when I got home, I realized there wasn't enough food in the bag to cook a meal. And, to top it off, now everyone I had listed on that paperwork was aware of just how bad off we were.

To make things worse, R.J. was getting ready to start school. I didn't even have enough money to feed the boys properly, so how in the world was I going to afford school clothes and supplies? I sat on the couch the Sunday before R.J. was to start school, feeling as helpless as I'd ever felt. I cried as my heart broke for my kids and for us, feeling completely helpless. But once again, fate intervened with a knock on the door. On my porch were two beautiful angels, Artis' mother, Linda Chappell, and Rosie Roberts, our sons' first babysitter, with school clothes and supplies. I couldn't believe it as I cried and cried, but now with joy. Somehow, someone had known exactly what we needed when we needed it, and we'd made it through yet again.

And then I got a bit angry. Just making it through wasn't good enough! I was supposed to have a successful life, to be like my parents. We were supposed to be making happy memories. Why was I struggling to even have school supplies for my kids? That's not a happy memory. I knew my parents must have struggled and I remembered that growing up, we didn't have much money, but we still had plenty of fun. Our parents put effort into creating happy memories for us, and I didn't feel like I was doing that for my family.

I decided then and there that my father had raised a girl who had always gotten what she wanted, and my mother certainly hadn't raised a failure. I was going to make it through this someway, somehow — for me, for my husband and for my boys.

When You Fail to Plan, You Plan to Fail

For me, winning isn't something that happens suddenly on the field when the whistle blows and the crowds roar. Winning is something that builds physically and mentally every day that you train and every night that you dream. – Emmitt Smith

We worked so many hours, Artis and I, and spent so much time with the boys that there was hardly any time for just us. Any moment we could be together was important to us. Yes, we were stressed out. We were strained financially. Years of struggling were putting tension on our relationship and were sometimes hindering our ability to be good parents. And, truly, Artis and I were opposites. But the one thing we had in common was that we were committed to making our marriage work. We had to keep our family together, no matter what.

Artis was putting in long hours working multiple jobs and I worked where I could, but we weren't getting any enjoyment out of our life and we weren't getting anywhere fast. Artis did his best to keep our heads above water and I again began to look for employment that would help pay the bills. Any job, no matter how small, short-term, or low paying, was a job. It was up to me to make it more than that.

If you think about your philosophy in life and look at the actions you take each day, it's so important to remember that hard work pays off — even if at times it doesn't feel like it. I've always been a believer in that idea. It was just one of the many lessons I had learned from my parents and grandparents. Always put everything you have into everything you do, regardless of the task. Sometimes, I thought Artis and I worked as hard as we did because we had no choice. But in reality, we did have a choice. We could have chosen to fail. We could have chosen to just roll over and let life happen to us. But we didn't. We chose to take the little opportunities presented to us and use them to our advantage as best we could.

Many people today believe they deserve to start a job at a higher position than they are offered, but we all need to remember there is nothing wrong with starting at the bottom and working your way up. I have thought that way my entire life; I don't care where you start me out; I'm going to end up at the top. At certain points in my life, it seemed that my efforts were futile and I wanted to give up. But I kept moving forward, one small step after another, hoping and praying it would pay off.

It's often been said that small steps bring great rewards. You never really know when a small break will be the stepping-stone to fantastic opportunities. I saw an ad in the paper for a billing clerk/receptionist for a pager company. I knew I had a dynamic personality and a go-getter attitude and thought I could really be great as a receptionist. And, of course, it was a much-needed job. I called the number and set up a time to be interviewed. I met with a lovely lady named Linda Christensen and was hired on the spot. The company was Parkway Communications and the position paid $6.00 an hour. It wasn't the highest paying job, but it was a job and, like any job, there was always opportunity to work my way up the ladder. Up until that time, pagers had been used mostly on job sites, like in hospitals. But in the early 90's wide-area paging was invented and introduced to the public. Parkway was trying to expand consumer pager usage in the Dallas area. And I was there to help them make it happen. My work ethic wouldn't allow me to just sit back and watch, regardless of my position.

When I started at Parkway I immediately began watching, listening and learning from the managers in the building. I always offered my assistance, regardless of the task, and gradually learned the responsibilities of each position. I worked really hard, and for the first time, my hard work was paying off. My work ethic and attitude had caught the attention of my managers, and I quickly began to work my way up the ladder, eventually landing a coveted sales position.

Unfortunately, my grandmother fell ill just as I began to make my mark in sales, and my mother and I travelled back and forth to the hospital every day to visit her. My grandmother, Helen Allen, had been a constant presence in my life growing up. She was a strong, giving woman who had taught me many of my most valuable childhood lessons. She lived a modest life, but was always willing to share what she had with us and anyone else who needed it. It was important to her that her grandchildren learn to give whatever we had to whoever needed it, regardless of how little we had ourselves. If someone was hungry, you fed him, even if it was your last piece of bread. If someone was cold, you clothed them, even if it was your only coat. By doing this, you would receive what you needed when you needed it most. My grandmother was an inspiration to my mother in the same way my mother was to me. I could barely stand the pain I was going through watching my grandmother slowly slip away, and I could only imagine what my mother was enduring. In those last days, my mother comforted my grandmother, promising that she would never be forgotten, that we would find a way to celebrate her life and to honor her memory.

When my grandmother passed away, the vice president of Parkway, Rick Bush, drove me from the office to my mom's house. He was paying his condolences to me and telling me to take what time I needed and, in almost the same breath, told me that the director of marketing, Pam Porter, had resigned. Pam was a strong businesswoman. She had taught me a lot, and I wondered who would take her place. To my surprise, Rick announced that upon my return, they wanted me to take the position. Once again, the highs and lows of life kicked in. My sorrow over the passing of my grandmother weighed on one side of the scale, and my excitement over my new position helped balance the other.

Somehow this simple high school graduate with no formal sales experience or education in marketing had made her way up to director of marketing. I was ready for the challenge. There were 72 employees and six stores under me. And I was making $60,000 a year. What an unbelievable change! Artis and I could finally shop for groceries without having to worry about whether we had enough money left to pay the light bill. A very heavy weight had been lifted off my shoulders, but not without a lot of hard work and dedication to excellence. As the marketing director, it was part of my job to make and keep personal connections in the Dallas area. I began to learn that you never know when somebody can help you make the next sale or when you will have the opportunity to help out someone else. A chance meeting would lead to something great. While I was working for Parkway, I got wind about the upcoming grand opening of Drew Pearson's Sports Bar & Grill. Drew was a former Dallas Cowboy who had helped take the team to three Super Bowls. He had retired from football in 1983, been a sportscaster for both CBS and HBO and was CEO of Drew Pearson Companies, a manufacturer of licensed headgear. I knew there would be a lot of people there to market our services to, so imagine my surprise when we received a fax and my name was on their VIP guest list.

As usual, I had my stack of business cards ready to go and was introducing myself to everyone I came in contact with. One person I gave my card to was Dallas Cowboys football star Emmitt Smith. Yes, *the* Emmitt Smith. I confidently introduced myself and told him, "If you ever need a pager, please call me." He asked, "What would I need a pager for?" I told him he never knew who would need to get in touch with him, explained how the service worked and left it at that. I was cool and confident on the outside, but inside I was jumping up and down screaming with excitement. I went to the office the next day and was just going on and on about how I'd met Emmitt Smith and was sure I was going to be able to sell him our services. I told everybody in the office, in the stores; I was just so excited. But days went by and I didn't hear anything. My bubble burst and I thought that I wasn't going to hear from him. I began to give up hope. Then, one day, the receptionist buzzed into my office saying Emmitt Smith was on the phone. I really thought the girls in the office were playing a joke on me, so I picked up the phone expecting to hear my receptionist faking a man's voice. Boy was I surprised when it really was Emmitt calling to say he wanted to know more about our pager services. I sold our services like I'd never sold before, highlighting our superior customer service and that we had the Cadillac of pagers for him. Emmitt was sold. Pat me on the back for another sale.

Shortly after making that sale, I was in a meeting with Rick Bush and his brother, George, the president of the company (not the country). All at once, Rick blurted out a crazy idea. The concept was for Emmitt to record a statement to the effect of, "Hey, this is Emmitt Smith and I carry a Parkway Pager" that people would hear while they waited on hold. Everyone around the table thought it was a great idea, but impossible. But I said, "Okay, well, how about I get it done?" Both Rick and George laughed in disbelief. "There's no way, Cheryl," said George. After all, Emmitt was a superstar in Dallas. "Well," I said, "what will you do if I do get it done?" After all, this would be a big deal and I should get something, right? "I'll buy you a big screen TV," said Rick. Rick sounded pretty confident that I couldn't do it. That was all the challenge I needed. So, I picked up the phone to call Emmitt. I explained to him what Parkway wanted to do. He referred me to the promotions company in charge of arranging those types of things for him. I spoke to the contact Emmitt had given me and the gentleman wanted to know how much we were willing to pay. When I explained we were hoping Emmitt would just do it because he was a customer, the gentleman flatly told me no way, no how. After a few days passed, though, Emmitt called and asked what the promotional company had said. When I explained the conversation, Emmitt responded, "Cheryl, don't worry about it. I'll do it." And when I told Emmitt that if he did the recording I would get a big screen TV, he said, "You'd better get the biggest screen TV you can get!" Emmitt completed the recording for me, singing the praises of Parkway Pagers for all our customers to hear. And I got the biggest screen TV I could find, courtesy of Rick Bush. I still have that TV to this day.

As fate would have it, that Cadillac of pagers I sold Emmitt broke down and he called me and asked to have his pager replaced. I told him I would bring by a new pager to his office right away. When I got to the office, Emmitt began asking me about paging services, what it was about, how much money could be made in communications. I explained to him all about it and he asked me if I'd be willing to bring him a business plan on the concept. I told Emmitt I would get it done for him and bring it back. Of course, I was working hours upon hours per week, travelling all over the area making sales plus taking care of my family, so I didn't really have the time to devote to writing a business plan at that moment. Plus, why would this man want me to put together this plan for him? He could pay any number of marketing geniuses to do that.

About a month later, I got another phone call. A deep, smooth voice said to me, "Ms. Jackson, this is Horace Irwin. Mr. Smith would like the business plan for the paging company, and I need it on my desk by Monday." Something about the way this man spoke told me he was a serious business professional with a lot of savvy, and that it would be a good idea to honor his request. I immediately said, "Yes, sir." I worked hard and fast to put together a business plan for introducing a new communications company based on paging services. I presented the plan to Mr. Irwin, and to my delight and relief, he was thoroughly impressed. He took the plan to Emmitt, who was just as impressed, and Mr. Irwin set up a meeting for us.

I discovered Emmitt was a very down-to-earth guy. He was a people person, passionate about football and full of hopes and dreams. I had the opportunity to meet his family, which was always so important to him, a quality I related to. He was very caring about his good name and what it represented. He had worn the number 22 on his football jersey since his college days, still had that number as a Dallas Cowboy, and made certain every action he took represented his number favorably. He knew folks would connect that number with him and he was determined to leave a legacy. He was focused on his goals and what he wanted to achieve in his life. I was impressed with Emmitt and inspired by his enthusiasm and business smarts. He really was an ordinary man leading an extraordinary life. So I signed on to work with him to bring this plan to fruition. I left Parkway Communications and my high paying job and set to work with Emmitt in forming Emmitt Smith Communications. It was a leap of faith.

Emmitt was a true businessman, and as he started to lay the plans and build the deals to launch this new venture, he brought me along to sit in on those important meetings. He opened me up to a whole new world in business. With Emmitt, I had the opportunity to sit across the table from people like the presidents of AT&T and Motorola and learn the fundamentals of entrepreneurship and negotiations. He taught me how to really build relationships and hold onto them. He was swinging some crazy business deals and I was learning a lot about business, my abilities and myself along the way. Emmitt was convinced of the power behind stating your goals in order to achieve them. He knew he had to set specific goals and really believe in them in order to make them come true. He told me all about wanting to make it into the Pro Football Hall of Fame. He was determined to break the all-time rushing record. But Emmitt was also a philanthropist in the true sense of the word. Anytime Emmitt would agree to an engagement where he would sign autographs, he required the thousands of people who lined up to bring a non-perishable food item or new toy in exchange. I learned through him just how much someone can use their life to impact the world we live in and the people who live in it. Everywhere we went together, I was in awe of his generosity. My own family even benefited from his kindness. He would bring big boxes of barely worn shoes he had worn in games or to church and tell me to take them home and give them to my husband and my sons. To this day, we still have some of those shoes.

Emmitt Smith Communications continued to expand, and as telecommunications evolved, we evolved with it. Emmitt worked a deal with AT&T Wireless to provide cellular services, and one of my jobs was to help find new corporate contracts. A concept we came up with was to partner with local car dealerships to offer cellular phone service to purchasers of new vehicles. One of the dealerships we partnered with was Middlekauff Ford. When someone would purchase a new vehicle from Middlekauff, they would receive a certificate for a free cellular phone from Emmitt Smith Communications. Once they qualified for service, they received their free phone. Together, Emmitt and I built his company into a success and my business savvy evolved as a result.

But as much as I enjoyed working for Emmitt, eventually it was time for me to move on. Artis and I had decided that the time had come for me to stay at home for a while. I had been working so hard for so long, and it was good timing. Artis was doing well in his job and we had the means for me to fulfill that part of my family obligations. Emmitt and I severed our business relationship, but have remained friends. I learned one-on-one lessons in both giving and achievements from Emmitt Smith that will last me the rest of my life. I was blessed to work with one of the country's greatest philanthropists and to learn from him how to truly use my life to make a difference and take everything I do to a higher degree of excellence. I will never forget my experiences with Emmitt and will forever be grateful to him for what he taught me, what I learned and the connections I made. I still keep in contact with Emmitt and his strong, beautiful wife, Pat. And to his credit, the people I met while working for the great Number 22 helped me in my journey to success for years to come and continue to help me to this day.

Reflecting back, everything that Emmitt Smith said he would achieve — every goal, every dream — he conquered. He talked about it, he put plans together, he followed those plans and he achieved his goals. On October 27, 2002, on the big screen television that Emmitt Smith had negotiated for me, I watched him become the NFL's all-time leading rusher. And later, on that same television, I watched him become the winner of "Dancing with the Stars." His dance partner's name was Cheryl.

If You Believe It, Claim It

Do your little bit of good where you are; it's those little bits of good put together that overwhelm the world. – Bishop Desmond Tutu

My mother had made a promise to my grandmother Helen that her life would be celebrated and her memory honored. After years of being a pastor, my father was called to begin his own ministry and, together with my mother, established DayStar Deliverance Ministries. One of the ministries my mother started at DayStar was The Touch Ministry, now known as Helen's House, to honor my grandmother Helen Allen. Since I was now staying home with the boys, I helped my mother begin this wonderful outreach for those in need. It was a special way to truly honor my grandmother, and my mother would always say, "I wish my mother could see this." With so many activities for my mother as a pastor's wife and now a bishop of the church, she gave me the responsibility of marketing The Touch Ministry so she could keep her promise to her mother.

DayStar Deliverance and The Touch Ministry were completely dedicated to helping those in need. That had been the tone of my parents' entire life when we were growing up, so it was no surprise to me they were continuing those efforts in their own church. Only, it must have increased tenfold. My parents were constantly looking out for others; food and clothing drives, youth programs and financial assistance. You name it, they did it. Mom and Dad were a true inspiration to my family and me, and we always tried to mimic their philanthropy as best we could, but really couldn't ever come close to their level of benevolence. They were so giving in their ministry and in their lives; they were truly touched by God. Of course, God works in mysterious ways.

My parents had been planning a huge community outreach event, and Artis and I had been very deeply involved in the planning. Days before the event was scheduled to take place, a huge storm blew through Dallas. The wind howled all night long and we watched the news as reports of destruction came over the TV. We thought to ourselves that our outreach event was going to be bigger than we anticipated because all these people were going to need help and they would need it immediately. We began to wonder if we had enough food, clothing and personal items for such a large crowd. We went to bed that night knowing the next day would be full of phone calls and a last ditch effort to pull in more donations for the community.

The next morning, when my parents arrived at the church, they discovered a shocking site. The destruction we had seen on the news hadn't just happened to others in the community — it had happened to us, too. The roof of the church was partly blown away and the remainder had caved in completely. Everything that had been stored up for the outreach event — food, clothing and household items — had been destroyed. The roof was lying on top of it all and what hadn't been landed on was completely soaked and windblown. The entire scene looked like something out of a movie, and we stood there in disbelief. Why had this happened? How could God allow this to happen to people who were so dedicated to helping His children? What in the world were we going to do for all those in the community who were counting on us to provide for them, especially now? If there was ever a faith-shaking event, this was it. But not for my parents. They immediately jumped into action, calling their insurance company to find out what they were supposed to do next. Mom gathered groups of volunteers together to start sorting through the mess to see if anything was salvageable. Very little was. It was a devastating blow. But that wasn't the half of it.

The insurance company came out immediately to take a look at the damage and informed my father that the roof, and all the collateral damage, was not covered by the church insurance policy. Were they kidding? What was the point of insurance if it wasn't going to cover what you needed when you needed it? I'm not sure my parents knew quite what to do at that point. It was going to cost tens of thousands of dollars to repair the damage to the roof and the interior of the church. The church had some money and we were certain the congregation would give what they could, but it wasn't a wealthy church, by any means. Typical of my parents, though, they focused their attention on what they were going to do to provide goods for the outreach event. They still planned on holding it, church or no church, and got on the phone, calling everyone they could think of to scrounge up more donations. Of course, at this point, we needed more than just the food and clothing and such. We needed the basics, like tables and chairs.

I realized that I might be able to use some of my contacts with the Dallas Cowboys to get some donations coming in. I called around and eventually got hold of Michael Irvin, the Cowboys' All-Pro receiver. I explained the situation, and he offered to help out in any way he could, whether it be donations or promoting the event. He offered to come to the event and started to make his own phone calls to solicit help while I continued to wrack my brain for ideas. There was no way I was going to turn that offer down!

I have a tendency to be known as someone who isn't ashamed to beg and plead for what I need. Not what I need for my personal life, mind you, but for charity. That's what I was doing that day. I was pouring my heart out on the phone to anyone I could reach, letting them know the desperate situation we were in. I remembered meeting Larry Jones, the founder of Feed the Children, when I worked with Emmitt. When I called Larry, he immediately agreed to help us. The organization had been known for years for delivering food, medicine, clothing and other necessities to needy children in the U.S. and across the world. They were headquartered in Oklahoma City, but Larry offered to drive down and give us the help we needed.

The response was overwhelming. We had donations flooding in to replace the destroyed items, and Larry Jones showed up with a huge tractor-trailer full of food for distribution. Every media outlet in the city was there to cover the event and, once again, Mother was saying, "I wish my mom were here to see this." It was a marvelous sight. Michael Irvin was working the crowd because word had gotten out he would be there, and people were showing up not only to receive, but also to give. The whole event was a huge success, despite the destruction that lay in the background.

We still had to figure out what we were going to do about the roof and damage to the church. There was just no way my parents and the congregation could do this on their own. Artis and I discussed it, and decided to make a huge sacrifice for the sake of my parents and the church. Artis had about $10,000 put away in his 401(k) at his job. It was all we had set aside for retirement, but retirement seemed so far away, we thought we could give up that money to help repair the roof. Our budget was tight again since I had stopped working, but we were still managing to get by. Artis could just continue making the contributions to his retirement fund out of each check and we would start over from zero. The lessons my parents had taught me were coming full circle. We were giving every penny we had to help the church and its members.

My parents protested at first when we told them what we were doing. Honestly, I protested, too, when I realized we would be broke. I repeatedly tried to talk Artis into making smaller donations to the church so we wouldn't be completely without, but he insisted that God had told him to give it all. After much begging and pleading, I realized there was nothing I could do by myself to change his mind. So I put together a meeting with my parents, where we all sat down to talk Artis out of giving away all our money. While my mother was arguing with him, Artis looked at her and said yet again, "God told me to do this." My mother looked at me, and I immediately knew that I might as well stop kicking her under the table. There was nothing any of us could do or say to talk my husband out of this bold, courageous leap of faith. This was as much our church as it was theirs, and we had been so blessed to have people rescue us at just the right moments throughout our marriage. Artis felt it was our turn to do something for someone else. It was terrifying, but once we took the plunge, it also felt good.

Artis went to work and asked for the money out of his 401(k) retirement plan in order to put it into the roof repairs. Unfortunately, back in those days, the rule was you couldn't pull money from an existing plan unless you no longer worked for the company. So Artis fixed that problem in order to get the money. Imagine my surprise when he walked in the door from work that night and announced he had quit! Quit? Just like that? With nothing to fall back on and very little in savings, we were now both unemployed. I asked Artis, "Exactly what do we do now?" Artis said he would start his own company. He had worked those early years for his father in landscaping and was confident he could run his own company. Granted, he was good at what he did and was a very hard worker, but it didn't really make sense to me to begin a company without having another income coming in. We didn't have much of a choice at that point, though. What was done was done.

Thankfully, I had all those contacts I had made while working for Emmitt Smith. I began working my rolodex and knocking on doors on Artis' behalf, trying to help him land contracts for landscaping and maintenance. One of the doors I knocked on was Middlekauff Ford. I went to see the general manager of the dealership, Earl Hudson, whom I had worked closely with when working the deal with Emmitt Smith Communications. I pestered Earl until we had negotiated an agreement for Artis to provide landscaping services to Middlekauff. It was a fantastic opportunity for Artis, and I was happy to be able to help push his new company. Middlekauff was his first contract.

Another relationship I capitalized on to help Artis get his company off the ground was Troy Aikman Ford. I had met Troy on a business level while working with Emmitt. Troy was the quarterback for the Dallas Cowboys and had led the team to four consecutive NFC Championship games — along with Emmitt, of course. Like Emmitt, Troy was a people person, a down-to-earth guy. I approached Troy at his dealership with a proposal for Artis' new company to take over the landscaping and maintenance. I gave my pitch, we worked out the numbers and settled on a contract.

Not long after, I was at a Dallas Mavericks game and Troy and his wife were sitting a few rows in front of me. I guess I must have cleaned up pretty well, because Troy looked at me with surprise and said, "What are you doing here?" I guess maybe because I was the maintenance man's wife, it took him by surprise. I just smiled and waved and thought to myself, "I'm supposed to be here." That's an important thing to keep in mind. Those words "I am supposed to be here." Sometimes people may question you verbally or with a look, or even a scowl, but it's important that you just know you are walking in the perfect plan that God has for you and that every meeting, every event and everything special, you deserve. Don't let anyone question your motives or whether you "deserve" something or not.

Even with the contracts I was helping Artis pick up for his new company, things were really getting tight financially. While Artis was working the contract for Middlekauff, a man named Mark mentioned a need for another receptionist and asked Artis if he thought I would be interested. I was still dedicated to staying home with the kids, but the additional money was needed, so I agreed to work the receptionist desk part-time. I started out that April making $9.00 an hour. Very quickly it was apparent to me the other receptionists just didn't take their jobs seriously. More and more frequently one of the other two girls would call in sick or not show up, and I would be asked to come in to cover for them. My work ethic just wouldn't allow me to do a job halfway and I eventually began working full-time as the other receptionists were let go.

By August, I was making $11.50 an hour because I was essentially doing the jobs of three people. I was working more than full-time, opening the doors at 6:30 a.m. and closing the dealership at 10 p.m. I was dedicated to doing my work the correct way and was committed to being successful, no matter what the job. As a result, just four months later, I was given another raise to $13.50 an hour and given the additional duties of being in charge of customer service. That was a large amount of money, in my opinion, just for running a switchboard and taking care of customer issues. Once again, a small opportunity had turned into a larger one through hard work. I was soon promoted to customer relations director and received another raise in February to a salary of over $36,000 per year.

Soon after, I had great support from the staff and assembled a fantastic team of people to work with and for me. Phyllis Logsdon was Ric Middlekauff's secretary, and she was always very supportive of me. I miss the mornings when Phyllis would say, "Let's go have some coffee," and I would pour myself a cup of coffee even though I don't drink it. We would laugh about that every time. It's extremely important to have someone you can talk to and confide in, and Phyllis was that person for me as I made my way up the ladder at the dealership. I was lucky enough to develop a team of people who respected me, listened to me and bent over backwards to help achieve my goals and the goals of the dealership. It's always great to have support, but many times it takes much more than that to realize a dream. It takes courage, persistence and determination.

Roger Adams was someone who could tell you all about determination. I had met Roger at the dealership, and he struck me as brilliant right away. He was a unique man whose parents had owned a roller skating rink when he was growing up and had learned to skate at a very young age. Roger impressed me for several reasons. He had a dream and wasn't going to let anyone sway him from that.

Roger had been a clinical psychologist and had been promoted to being a mental health supervisor while living in Oregon — he'd hated it. He had gone through a divorce, was on call constantly, and was just burned out and bummed out. While on vacation, he had been watching all the kids go up and down the beach on their inline skates and got a bit nostalgic for his youth. And then he came up with a dazzling idea. Why not make a sneaker that could convert into a roller skate? He had immediately come up with a prototype by taking a pair of sneakers, cutting out part of the bottom and inserting a rod and skateboard wheel. And his concept was born.

Roger had been working on prototype after prototype, and he would bring each new design in for Ric Middlekauff to see. I was always amazed at what he was doing as he continued to tweak the design. He would show Phyllis and me the improvements he had made and then add, "Now, I need to change this and move this and maybe I need to add this." Roger was trying to perfect his product and, at the same time, was shopping the idea around to major shoe manufacturers. Ric was very supportive of Roger and had given him some funds to help develop his prototypes. Roger was determined to make this a success, despite the fact that every one of the companies he had approached had turned him down. Many of his friends and family told him it was a foolish idea, nobody was going to buy it and he was going to fail. By this time, Roger was broke and homeless and figured he had nowhere to go but up. Each time Roger would come into the dealership, I would ask him if someone had bought his idea. "No, not yet," he would reply. That didn't matter to Roger. He knew he was going to make it.

It doesn't matter what idea you have or what you want to accomplish. Only one person needs to believe that you will succeed and that person is you. It may take years for you to reach your goal, but persistence is the key. Roger believed in himself and he continued to shop his idea around to shoe companies, until he finally decided he would just produce the shoes himself. Mr. Middlekauff invested in Roger's idea. I didn't have money to give him, but when Roger opened up his office I helped make it look more professional by taking him "shopping" in my house. I gave him a waterfall and some pictures to hang on the walls; whatever he needed he could have. Roger was extremely thankful to both of us, and he told me that he would one day be able to repay the favor.

Roger set up his office, created his company and found a production facility to create his flagship product — the Heely. He introduced his product at a trade show that year, made his first sale, and the store that carried the first Heelys sold out in just hours. Several years later, Roger's company went public. Heelys are now sold in more than 30 countries and his company employs over 700 people. They come in multiple styles, one or two-wheeled versions and different types of wheels for various experience levels. Roger's company even built six specially sized pairs of Heelys for Shaquille O'Neal — in a size 22. In a 2004 interview with MSNBC, Roger told of his struggle to succeed and the naysayers that had surrounded him. "There's a magic to believing in something," he said. "If I'd listened to the many people saying, 'No, you can't do this,' I'd have never gotten off square one." I couldn't have said it better myself.

My previous sales jobs were great experiences for me for later in life, because selling anything means you have to sell yourself. If the customer believes in you and believes you are genuine, they'll be more likely to buy something from you. That philosophy was put to the test the day football star Deion Sanders drove into the dealership. Actually, I saw him as he was driving out of the dealership. Apparently, he had come into the showroom to pick out a car, but the salesperson hadn't given him the deal he wanted. I flagged him down as he was getting ready to drive out of the parking lot and asked him to give me the opportunity to earn his business. I had previously met Deion at the grand opening of Emmitt Smith Communications, and I had sold him two cellular phones. I reminded him of our first meeting and assured him that I could take care of his needs. Deion told me what he wanted to pay for his vehicle and I took him in, gave him everything he wanted, and made the deal. Deion became my ambassador that day. He went out and told everyone he knew about me, and what a great salesperson I was. I had people coming in left and right to buy vehicles from me because that's what Deion Sanders had told them to do.

As fate would have it, I ended up in a very familiar situation not long after that encounter. We were all in a meeting, and the subject came up of how great it would be to have Deion Sanders do a commercial for us. Sound familiar? It did to me, and as Ric Middlekauff laughed and said how impossible it would be, I asked him what he would do for the person who could get Deion to do the commercial. Hey, you have not because you ask not. Life is a give and take. If you give, you should expect it to come back to you in one form or another.

So, I went to Deion and I asked him if he would do the commercial for us. He laughed at first, but just like I did with my father when I was little, I asked him again and again until he finally broke down and said, "Okay, Cheryl, I'll do the commercial." So I brought Deion in to meet with Mr. Middlekauff, and he said he would do the commercial on one condition: that I was in the commercial with him. When you do, it comes back to you. I had never, in my wildest dreams, thought I would be involved in something like that. I was still adhering to my strict upbringing and didn't wear a stitch of makeup. Not the norm for being on camera, and I was excited for the opportunity. We ended up doing two commercials, Middlekauff Ford rewarded me nicely for getting Deion to participate — and I got a bit bitten by the camera bug.

Blind Faith

One evening, as Artis and I were out to eat with my parents, they happily announced to us they had been approved to buy a new home. They were so excited, and so was I. Not just for them, but for us. Artis' and my credit was so bad from our many years of struggling that, even though we were leading a better life financially, we knew we would never qualify to buy another home. We were still renting and I had told my mother over and over that if they ever moved I wanted to buy the house from her and Dad. I knew that house had to be mine. It was the house I had grown up in and it was the house I wanted. I begged my mom, pleaded with her, to give us their house. My mom looked across the table at me and said, "Cheryl, God has something so much better planned for you. Trust me." Excuse me? My mother had decided to give the house to my baby sister, Lynette. I couldn't believe it! My mom knew I was making good money and could afford to pay them for the house. She also knew how bad our credit was. How could she just give the house to Lynette? I was all at once jealous of both my parents and my sister. Mom told me that the house across the street from their new place was going to be going up for sale and that Artis and I would get that house. She knew the house would be coming on the market because the owner had told her she wanted to move back home to the Philippines.

"Mom, be real," I said. "How on earth do you think we're going to be able to get that house?"

Her response was simple. "God will provide," she said.

My parents had given me the address of their new house, so I drove by one day after work. If I wasn't jealous before, I sure was then. I was blown away. It was a gorgeous home, the kind of house we'd always dreamed of living in as kids but knew we could never afford. I was wondering if my parents had money socked away somewhere they hadn't told us about. Not so, I learned. It was another story of faith.

My parents had been looking for a new house and had come across this one in their search. They knew it was out of the realm of possibility to come up with the money for the down payment plus the money for closing, but they looked anyway. They met the owners of the house, and after many conversations with them, the owners told my parents they wanted them to be the new owners. They even went so far as to offer to pay for closing costs to get them into the house. My parents had been givers all their adult lives and had always trusted that God would provide for them. The way my parents saw it, this was God's way of thanking them for trusting in Him and for giving so much to His people.

As I was checking out my parent's new place, I turned to look at the house across the street that my mother had mentioned. Oh, wow. That place was just as amazing. Again I thought to myself, *how in the world does my mother think we're going to get that place?* It was one thing for God to provide for and reward my parents. They had lived true lives of faith. I had gone to church faithfully, but just because I was always in church didn't mean the church was always in me. I had serious doubts, so I put the thought out of my head and went on my way.

One day as I was visiting, my parents at their new home, my mom said, "C'mon Cheryl, let's go. I want to introduce you to the lady across the street." She grabbed my hand and led me out the front door. Adora Cox was a four-foot-seven, beautiful little lady. Mom told Adora that she wanted me to buy her house. She said, "Cheryl, meet the owner of your new house." Adora and I sat down to speak and she said she'd love for me to buy the house and I told her I'd love to buy it. She told me to go get the financing and the house would be mine.

Artis and I knew we couldn't do it, but it didn't stop us from trying. And trying. And trying again. We put in applications at every bank and mortgage broker we could find, all to no avail. We were making the money, but our credit was so messed up that the lenders had no choice but to turn us down. My mother kept telling us not to worry about it — God would provide. I had to admit, though, our faith was waning.

One Sunday, my mother was preaching in the church. As part of her sermon she said, "Whatever you want from God, if you really have faith and you believe it, then you go and you stand on it. You claim it!" Artis and I got in the car after church and looked at each other. I said, "Are you thinking what I'm thinking?" He said he was. So we drove right over to that house across the street from my parents. We got out of the car and we both stood on the grounds of that house. We pointed at that house, and we claimed it.

This was some blind faith. I had always been a believer but, like I said, I had been shaken in my faith a time or two (or ten). Would God? Could He? Artis and I couldn't have been firmer in our beliefs that day. We knew that house would be ours. We had claimed it.

Not long after that, we met with Adora again. She said she was getting ready to leave for the Philippines for a few months to build her new house there. "If you can't come up with the financing to buy this place," she said, "then I have no choice but to put the house on the market." She had spoken with her realtor and was confident the house would be sold before she came back. We were devastated. In fact, I was livid. Mother had told me that house was mine, to have faith and that God would take care of it. I was disappointed and angry. I asked God so many questions. Why couldn't we have it? We had faith; we had claimed it. Wasn't that supposed to be enough?

Artis and I went back to going about our day-to-day lives, giving no more thought to acquiring the house of our dreams. We knew it would be sold and that was all there was to it. It did creep up in my thoughts now and then and I could feel my frustration at the situation begin to build, so I'd quickly push the thought away. Weeks went by and I forgot all about the house. But about two-and-a-half months later, I got a phone call from Adora. I was surprised to hear from her and she asked me something that surprised me even more. "Cheryl," she said. "Do you still want this house?" I about dropped the phone. Artis and I had been sure the house had been sold. Adora asked if Artis and I could come and meet with her. Artis came by my office to visit soon after, and when he walked through the door I practically jumped on him, rambling on about the conversation I'd just had.

That day I came to the realization that if you put something in God's hands, completely give it over to Him, then there is no reason to hound Him about it or be anxious. He will provide when He's ready to or He decides you're ready. I really wish I had learned that earlier in life. God will do what He promised you He will do, but it's also about giving and receiving. If you give, you will receive. If you do for others, things will be done for you. Call it faith, call it karma, call it whatever you want but it's true.

We headed straight to Adora's house that evening and she told us that, for whatever reason, her realtor had neglected to put the house on the market. The house had sat there for over two months with not a single potential buyer to come and take a look. I was convinced, and still am to this day, that was God's work. My mother had always said, "There are good ideas and there are God ideas." That was the best "God idea" that had ever happened to me. Adora told us she needed to get out of the house right away because she was ready to make the move back to the Philippines and asked what we thought we could do to buy it. We told her we really didn't have any options as far as financing was concerned. She said she thought she might have an idea and asked if we'd be willing to send her our bank statements. Of course we were, and we left with renewed hope.

I mailed the bank statements off and sat and waited to hear something back. After what seemed like an eternity, Adora called and asked if she could meet us at our house right away. I could tell from the conversation that she wanted to meet at our house on short notice just to see what kind of housekeepers we were and how well we maintained our home. This would give her an idea of how we would keep up her home. Word to the wise: keep your house tidy. Taking care of what God has given you could be extremely important. When Adora arrived at our house, she took a long look around, and with a look of satisfaction, said, "Okay. You can't get financed, so I'll do the financing for you. The house is yours."

That's who God is. Here this woman had a $350,000 house and she was going to finance it for us. My husband and I looked at each other in disbelief and began to cry. Adora said, "Cheryl, I saw you one day standing out front and pointing at my house. What were you doing?" We shared with her just what we had done that day and that, through her, God was honoring our prayers.

Whatever it is you want to do in your life, whatever you need, claim it. Take action, right now. Write down the things you need and desire.

Believe in it. We believed we would get the house, we claimed it, we forgot all about it and then God, in his timing, provided. Of course, now it was up to us to make it a reality. Adora agreed to help us, but we had to prove ourselves. She set a timeline for coming up with the down payment in order to finance us. She gave us six months to give her $35,000. We decided to split it into six payments; five payments of $6,000 each and one final payment of $5,000. It was a daunting task, but we were up for it.

We looked at our income and our expenses and saw that we didn't have nearly enough extra at the end of each month to be able to pay this amount each month while still paying our current rent and bills. We dissected our budget to find ways to cut back. There just wasn't room for enough movement to make a difference. We decided Artis would have to look for quick, one-time projects he could do around his regular contract schedule. Once again, we were praying for a miracle.

I don't know how, but it happened. Each month, Artis would pick up a big enough side job or extra project to make that monthly payment. It could be an additional project from a current client, or a side job through word of mouth. It didn't matter what it was, whether it was building a fence or an extra landscaping project, he would do it. Each month we got closer to getting our new home. Each side job was its own tiny little miracle. At the end of six months, we made that final payment. And Adora gave her blessing for us to move into our new home. We were ecstatic. We couldn't have been happier. We finally had our own house, our own home. A place our boys could grow up in and look back fondly on as their childhood home. A place they could come back to with their own children once they were grown and had families of their own. And we were right across the street from my parents, who were so very important to us all. We still live in that home today.

Whether you think you can or think you can't – you are right. – Henry Ford

The Power of Persistence

History shows us that the people who end up changing the world — the great political, social, scientific, technological, artistic, even sports revolutionaries — are always nuts, until they are right, and then they are geniuses. – John Eliot

The opportunities just kept coming from there. Ric Middlekauff paid to send his team leaders, including me, to a workshop in Detroit. One of the presenters at the conference was a man named Dr. Harry Cohen. Dr. Cohen touted himself as "a psychologist who doesn't believe in therapy." He was an independent management consultant, personal leadership coach and author with a very direct way of speaking to the workshop attendees. His message was simple, yet powerful. He told us authenticity and honesty breed trust. He stressed the importance of long-term growth and improvement. He spoke about using your life for the good of others, loving the people around you and building connections between people. He was all at once entertaining and sincere and inspiring. He was motivating the attendees to become the best they could possibly be as human beings. His words spoke to my soul. I was crying within the first ten minutes of hearing that man speak.

I was so moved by what Dr. Cohen and the other facilitators had done, I decided I wanted to do the same. I wanted to move people the way Dr. Cohen had moved me. When we got back from the conference, I spoke with Ric Middlekauff about what I wanted to do. Mr. Middlekauff was one of my biggest supporters, but he tried to give me a reality check. He pointed out the simple facts: I had no college education, no experience and it was a difficult industry to make it into. Basically, he was gently saying I wouldn't be able to do it because the odds were stacked against me. Once again, in my mind a challenge had been issued and there was no way I was turning it down.

I called Dr. Harry Cohen and told him I wanted to be a part of his team. I was very convincing and thought I had convinced him, too. Dr. Cohen explained to me that even if he wanted to, he couldn't hire anyone from Ford unless he received a letter recommending me and getting permission to hire — and even then he couldn't promise anything. But at least a letter of recommendation would get me in the door. I immediately went to Mr. Middlekauff's office and explained the situation to him. He could really see how much hearing the presenters at that conference had moved me. I desperately wanted to be a part of the electricity that was happening there in Michigan and knew I could add my own personal stories and experiences to the team. I told Mr. Middlekauff I would be thrilled if he would write the letter for me. Again, he tried to explain to me that I didn't have the qualifications for the job. I told him, "Sir, I believe you write the best letters of anyone I know. And I believe that if you write this letter of recommendation for me, there's no way I won't get this job."

Mr. Middlekauff had been so kind to my family and I knew he loved us. He would give his tailor-made shirts to me to give to Artis, shirts I never would have been able to afford to buy him. They always had "Ric" embroidered on the front, and to this day Artis still has some of those shirts. I can now afford to have the embroidery removed and have my husband's monogram put in their place, but I've left some of those shirts with "Ric" on them. You never want to forget where you came from, and the people who helped you along the way.

So, out of sheer love for my family and me, Mr. Middlekauff wrote that letter of recommendation. I immediately sent the letter off to Dr. Cohen and he arranged to fly me out to Detroit for an interview. I was even more convincing in that interview than I had been on the phone. I told my background, my stories and why I would be a good motivational speaker. I explained to Dr. Cohen how I could be an asset to his company. And then I made an astounding announcement, arrogant even. I informed Dr. Cohen that I could only work two days a week for him, three at the maximum. Taking this job would mean flying back and forth to Michigan, because I had no intention of uprooting my family. I must have made a convincing argument, despite my arrogance, because Dr. Cohen hired me on ... making an astounding $1695 per day.

It was a fantastic job. I was conducting workshops every week in Detroit and flying back to Dallas to spend time with my family. I loved what I was doing. I loved motivating people to do something better with their lives. It was a rewarding job and I worked with a fabulous group of people. I had the opportunity to spend some time with Dr. Cohen's wife, Jan, and we went together to see Oprah Winfrey's first "Live Your Best Life" tour when it came to Detroit. I hadn't really been an avid follower of Oprah up until that point, but I was interested in her philanthropic work. We had a fabulous time and I learned so much about Oprah's life that I never knew. We got to hear about her background and her upbringing, her life and her generosity. I was inspired by that generosity and how she was able to accomplish what she did on such a massive level. I began to identify with her a bit more. This woman had gotten to a point in her life that I aspired to and, knowing her background and the struggles she went through to get there, I could finally see myself achieving my goals.

Gradually, my two days per week in Detroit turned into three-day workshops, and those three-day workshops turned into four. I was spending more time in Michigan and flying across the country than I was at home. I began to feel like I was missing important parts of my sons' lives and missed moments shared with my husband. Money is great and often requires you to make sacrifices. But my family wasn't a sacrifice I was willing to make.

Thankfully, I learned very early on never to burn bridges. It had been beneficial to me throughout my life to leave with grace from any position I held, and I had always been able to go back and use the resources from previous jobs to help further my current career or my life. The same held true for my relationship with Middlekauff Ford, and when I asked to return to my previous position, I was welcomed with open arms. I was back to being able to work near my family, which I would never take for granted again. Despite the amount of money I had been making while working for Dr. Cohen, my family life had suffered greatly. I really missed a lot of my boys' day-to-day lives, activities and school events. I missed being with my parents. I wasn't as close to my husband. There had been a lot to gain from the job in Michigan, a found a wonderful mentor in Dr. Cohen who understood and applauded my decision to choose family, return home and I did just that.

It really did seem like I finally had it all: a beautiful family, loving parents, successful job and now a lovely home. I was living a good life. But, for some reason, I was growing increasingly restless. I was finally in the position, after years of struggling, to pay my bills, feed my family and live a comfortable existence. But maybe part of the problem was just that; I *existed*, but wasn't really living. I was still struggling with what exactly I really wanted to do with my life. I had thought that success would come easily. I'd get married, have kids, stay home to raise my children while my husband supported the family, and help out neighbors and the community when I could. Not exactly what my parents had done, and certainly not ministry, but something similar to how they had led their lives. That had been my idea of success. My views and ideas about success were now changing, evolving if you will. I was born to be a difference maker, to live my life with purpose. I needed something more.

As I was experiencing this transition, my faith in "God will provide" grew more and more. And with the growth of my spiritual faith came the growth of my belief in myself. I began to trust that little voice of intuition — call it "gut instinct" if you want — that would speak to me in my experiences, no matter how big or small. It was during this time of personal growth that I found out Sarah Ferguson, the Duchess of York, would be in town promoting a new line of china she had designed.

Anyone who knows my mother knows she has exquisite taste. She also collects unique china and silverware. She's always thought of those possessions as priceless beauty and will occasionally pull them out for a "spot of tea." It is always fun to see my mother go into her faux British accent and assume full character as she drinks from one of her favorite teacups. Some are trimmed in gold, some laced with pretty little flowers and all have a sturdy weight to them. These are definitely considered good china, but she never minds sharing coffee or tea in them with her everyday guests. Mother often points out what she loves the most about each piece of china she owns. She'll even go into the entire story of where she found it, what went into acquiring it, and whether it's part of a set.

Of course, knowing how much my mom loves tea, I decided I would go to the mall to buy a tea set and have it signed by the Duchess for my mom. I was not prepared for what I saw when I got there. The line to see the Duchess wrapped outside the mall doors and around the outside of the building for a mile or more. I stood patiently in line to get inside the store and purchase my tea set. I had just bought a brand new camera and brought it with me, because I was going to get a picture with the Duchess as well. But when I finally got to the front of the line to make my purchase, the woman at the counter advised me not to bother purchasing the tea set because they were going to have to cut the line off. She went on to say that there was no way I'd get to the table to have the Duchess sign it. I ignored her, of course. When you are on a mission, don't let anybody talk you out of what you have purposed to do. The lady behind the counter saw my camera and also informed me that the Duchess wouldn't be taking any pictures. That wasn't going to stop me either. I decided I would just have to find another way.

My sister-in-law, Chandra, was with me on this adventure, and after I finished purchasing my tea set we didn't go back to the end of the line. Instead, I pulled Chandra aside with me and we stood beside where the line was formed, but within earshot of the Duchess. I started saying, "Fergie! Fergie!" Chandra just looked at me like I was crazy, as usual. I'm sure she was wondering what on earth I was doing. People in line began to stare, but I didn't care. I knew what I was doing. I was going to get The Duchess' attention. Finally, the she began to look up every now and again in my general direction and I continued to sing her name. "Fergie! Fergie!" Everybody likes to hear their name. At one point, a woman in line looked at me and scornfully said, "She is not *Fergie*. She is the *Duchess of York*." "Well, I know her as Fergie," I said, and continued to call her name. As the Duchess looked up one more time, we made eye contact and I knew I was making progress. "Fergie! Fergie!" I continued to call. Between signing autographs, the Duchess called one of her security guards over to the table and whispered something to him. The security guard immediately headed our way. This was it, I thought. I'd gotten her attention. I was being brought over to meet the Duchess and have my mom's tea set signed. I waited excitedly as the guard approached us and said, "Ma'am, the Duchess has asked that you be removed from the premises."

Chandra's jaw dropped. Even I, an African-American woman, turned two different shades of red. I immediately began to apologize. I was mortified. I had no intention of offending the Duchess — I was only trying to get her attention. As I continued to apologize profusely, the security guard grabbed me by the arm with one hand and the red rope with the other. "Actually," he said with a smile, "She asked me to bring you to her. The Duchess really likes you."

Chandra lost it and began to yell and scream excitedly. This got the attention of everybody in line. They looked as if they wanted to know what made us "so special" that we were getting brought in ahead of everyone else. We were escorted to the table and the Duchess asked, "What is your name?" I introduced myself and she said, in her wonderful accent, "I have a best girl name Cheryl. What do you have there?" "I have your china," I said. "Will you sign it for me?" "Of course I will!" she exclaimed and she signed every single piece. Not only that, she happily agreed to have her picture taken with me. Mission accomplished.

I brought that tea set home to my mom and she cried with excitement. We still have that set and anytime we want to pretend we're rich, we pull out the tea set to sip our tea, pinkies raised.

I was learning to trust myself, and it was working. Listen to your intuition — and be persistent.

Big shots are only little shots who keep shooting. - Christopher Morley

Dream It, Speak It, Make It Happen

"You get in life what you have the courage to ask for." – Oprah Winfrey

I was sitting in the corner of our bedroom one day after working long hours, taking care of the boys and doing housework. I was irritated, angry at my life, exhausted and feeling completely defeated. I was tired of having a positive attitude when nothing seemed quite right. I had increased my involvement in the church, thinking maybe I hadn't been giving enough back. But that wasn't it. There really was something missing, and I just couldn't put my finger on it.

The television was on in the bedroom just as background noise to my private little pity party. "The Oprah Winfrey Show" was on, but I honestly wasn't paying much attention to it. I was too busy sulking. Then something caught my attention. Oprah was talking about how to truly be successful in your life. You have to claim success. You can't sit and wait for it to find you — you have to go after it. I had already done that with the house, my job, and the majority of the accomplishments in my adult life. Then I thought that maybe I wasn't really claiming what I wanted. I was sitting in the corner of the room feeling sorry for myself and angry about my situation, but what in the world was I going to do about it? I sat up and paid attention.

Oprah issued a challenge. "Make a list," she said. "Make a list of the ten things you want to do in life." *Okay, then what?* "Look at that list," she said, "and figure out what it takes to achieve those goals." Now, that spoke to my spirit. I had many friends, few enemies and much love, but there was still a void. Maybe I just hadn't defined what I really wanted to do and what I was supposed to be doing.

I generally didn't respond to things on TV, even from Oprah. I often thought about things I'd heard from her, but never really took specific action on them. Something about this really made me think, though. How many opportunities had I missed in my life? How many ways could I improve? And then I thought back to Emmitt Smith. He had a firm belief in the power of setting goals and setting out to accomplish them. I had learned so much from him, but it seemed that maybe I had missed one of the most important lessons.

I'm not sure what else Oprah said in that show, because I was already grabbing a pen and paper. I began to write down the things that I wanted most in life. As I wrote, tears began streaming down my face. I don't remember all the things that were on my list, but I do remember some of them.

Be a better wife and mother.

Have my own newspaper column.

Interview Oprah and be on the Oprah show.

Meet Denzel Washington.

Host my own radio show.

Host my own television show.

There. Now what? Oprah had asked what it would take to accomplish these goals. I knew what I needed to do to be a better wife and mother; it was fairly obvious to me. Time had flown by so fast, especially while I was traveling for my job in Detroit. I seemed to have lost a part of my boys while losing a part of myself. I needed to focus my efforts more on what I loved, as well as those I loved.

Next on the list, write a column for a newspaper. How was I going to achieve that? I was just a plain ol' girl from Dallas, Texas. I had no college education and no writing experience. The only experience I had in the newspaper industry was delivering papers with Artis. What newspaper on earth would give me my own column? After some days of deep soul searching and thinking about how to approach this goal, I decided I just needed to take action. I took a deep breath, mustered up my courage, picked up the phone and began calling different local newspapers. Call after call ended without even getting past the receptionist. That's when I realized the way I needed to do this was to get to the editors face to face. They had to see me and feel my energy to believe my words. So I began to go door to door.

After countless meetings with newspaper publishers, I walked into the office of Thurman Jones of *Minority Opportunity News,* also known as *MON the Gazette.* The paper was devoted to informing and educating the African-American community, promoting community events and encouraging people to become leaders. It tackled discrimination, racism, equal opportunity and business development. Not only was Mr. Jones the editor, he was the co-founder of the newspaper. He was also a high-ranking member of the Texas Publishers Association. This guy knew his stuff.

I sat in front of Mr. Jones and boldly told him what I wanted to do. I wanted my own column in his newspaper. Mr. Jones chuckled with his deep voice and asked me about my background. Everything I told him made it clearer and clearer that I was not college educated, nor did I have any writing experience and that he would be out of his mind to hire me. "So why should I give you a column?" he asked. "A lot of writers are trying to get in at this newspaper. Why you?"

I proceeded to tell him, with full authority, "Because I am going to interview Oprah Winfrey. And if you don't hire me, that article will appear in someone else's paper." I'm not sure where that statement came from but I knew, at that moment, I was going to get that interview. I sat there, proud and determined, and waited for his answer, fully expecting to be rejected but knowing for sure now that someone would hire me to write my column.

Mr. Jones looked squarely at me and laughed. I continued to look at him, just as serious as a heart attack. He smiled and asked me, "Okay, what would this column be about?"

I told him my column would be about *the plain truth*. I was going to interview people and have them tell me the plain truth about who they were, what they have done with their lives and what they wished they had done differently. "I'm going to interview people like Oprah who are giving back," I said. "And I'll interview the recipients and find out how they felt."

I really had a dream, as Martin Luther King, Jr., said. If I had thought too hard about what I was trying to do or if I hadn't believed in myself enough to go after it, that dream would never have become a reality. I had to listen to my heart. I dug deep down inside myself, decided what I wanted and went after it. I was claiming my own destiny. I sat in that office that day and waited to hear if my dream would be fulfilled at this newspaper, or if I had to move on to the next opportunity. Mr. Jones looked at me and said, "Okay, let's give it a try. You've got your own column."

Did I hear him correctly? Did he just say yes? Marvelous Mr. Jones had just helped make one of those dreams on my list of goals come true. He gave me the opportunity for my vision to come to fruition and be what I wanted to be in life. So I began to write.

I named my column, "The Plain Truth." I wrote articles about motivational and inspirational people in the community. People began telling me that they had read my column and they were proud of me. I was recognized for what I was doing, and that made me feel great.

The question still lingered, though: how would I interview Oprah?

I was discovering that if you have an intention and that intention lines up with your will, then amazing things can happen. It's about you doing something for yourself. If you fail to plan, you plan to fail. Now, I needed a plan for how to meet and interview Oprah.

Number One Fan

That's when the Oprah show decided to bring their second "Live Your Best Life" tour to Tampa, Florida. This was my opportunity! Sometimes in life you have to go outside of your comfort zone to get what you want. In order to achieve great things, you have to take a chance. Sometimes it's a big chance, a wild goose chase, a shot in the dark — whatever you want to call it. And from time to time, now and again, it pays off big.

Tickets to Oprah's "Live Your Best Life" tour that year were $185 each. I bought one and told my mom what I was doing. Oh, who am I kidding? I told everybody what I was doing! I told so many people that friends and family began to plan to go with me. They didn't have tickets to the show, mind you. They were just going along for the ride. There were a total of seven of us, and I had only three tickets. The others were going to stay in the hotel while I attended the tour.

I have always taken people along with me on my "adventures." It's never been about proving anything about me. It's more about showing what God can do if you give him the chance. I want people to truly understand that through Him all things are possible. A lot of persistence and a little bit of luck don't hurt, either. Before leaving for the tour stop, I decided I needed to do something to get Oprah's attention while at the conference. If I was going to have any chance of getting my interview, I would need to stand out. So I created a t-shirt that said "Oprah's #1 Fan" in big red letters. I was prepared for my first big opportunity. I called it my " Oprahtunity."

A group of us headed to Florida for our exciting journey. We got there early; in fact, three days early. I like getting places early because I can scope out the situation and get an idea of how things work, because you never know when somebody can help you out or vice versa. As we were checking into the hotel, I made eye contact and smiled at everyone I met. Two people I connected with were the concierge and the bell captain. These are the guys who are always in tune with everything that's going on.

They keep their ear to the ground and generally have some good info, but they don't share it with just anybody.

The morning Oprah was scheduled to present to the attendees, I donned my "#1 Fan" t-shirt under my red blazer. I had connected with the bell captain so many times that all I needed to ask him the day of the event was, "Yes or no?" The track of our conversation (and the translation) went something like this:
Me: Yes or no? (Is Oprah in the car everyone is running after and screaming at?)
Bell Captain: No. (That's the wrong car.)
Me: North, South, East or West? (Where's the real car?)
Bell Captain: North. (On the north side of the building in the secure parking garage.)

I knew from working for Emmitt Smith that celebrities hardly ever let people know which car they're in when the public has advance notice that they'll be at a particular location. It's not because they're stuck up or don't want to see their fans. Really, it becomes a huge problem getting anywhere on time when they have swarms of fans and press mobbed around the car, blocking the drive, knocking on the windows and trying to open doors. If they try to drive away in that mess, someone is liable to get hurt. So, there's usually a well-placed decoy car to divert everyone's attention while the real car slips out quietly. I headed north and intended to wait for Oprah's vehicle, so I could ask for my interview.

As I was getting ready to head over there, I overheard a man saying, "I need to meet Oprah. She has to hear my chicken story!" Something about the emotion and the passion in that man's voice convinced me that Oprah did, indeed, need to hear his chicken story. I knew I had to help him, so I asked, "Do you want to meet Oprah?" Of course he said yes, and so I told him to follow me. We introduced ourselves and he said his name was Jay. "Do you work for her?" he asked. "No, I don't," I said. "Just follow me." We headed out to the parking garage and stood at the security shack.

There was one security guard, one lead car and one limo. Jay was ecstatic. "I can't believe I'm going to meet Oprah," he said. "I've got my book; I'll sing my song and do my chicken dance for her!" That's right. This man was going to do a chicken dance for Oprah.

We waited for about twenty or thirty minutes, and then it began to rain. I had just had my hair done — I wanted to look good for my interview with Oprah, of course — so I tried to stay under the cover of the security shack. We spotted some movement start to happen, and the security guard told us it was time for us to move on and head across the street to the event. I looked out at the street and realized that if we had to move out from the cover of the security shack, then the only place we'd be able to stand would be in the median leading out to the main road that would take Oprah into the stadium. I looked at the median and the pouring rain and knew there was no way Oprah was going to stop the car to talk to two strangers standing in a median soaking wet, so I told Jay I was going to head across the street and find my seat in the stadium. I left and looked back to see Jay standing desperately in the median, waiting for Oprah's limo. He was determined.

I got inside the stadium and was finding my seat amongst the 2,000 people (mostly women) waiting to see Oprah. As I was waiting with anticipation for her to arrive, I began to hear my name being called across the stadium. It started out as just a whisper and at first I thought I was just hearing things. But it began to get louder. "Cheryl Jackson! Cheryl Jackson!" and I knew someone really was calling me. I look over to see Jay, soaking wet, waving frantically to get my attention, and he came running to me full speed. He had a few people with him, and as the group reached me they began excitedly asking, "You're the one who took him to meet Oprah?" I obviously had no idea what they were talking about until Jay breathlessly said, "Cheryl, she stopped the car. Oprah stopped the car!"

Oprah had stopped the car at that median. Jay had given her his book, sang his song and done his chicken dance in the rain. What a lesson for me that day. Sometimes your hopes will get rained on and sometimes people will try to stop you from achieving your dream. But when you have a belief that something is going to happen for you, you have to hold on firm. Jay believed and Jay stayed. Even though I was the one who led him to that opportunity, Jay made it happen for himself.

People around me heard the story and began to ask me if I was upset that I had walked away and Jay had gotten to meet Oprah. I wasn't too upset about it just then because I knew I would find a way to get my interview. When Lady Oprah herself stepped out onto the stage, the place erupted with cheers, and after the ruckus simmered down, Oprah immediately asked, "Where is Jay?" I just about fell over. "I want to have lunch with Jay," she said. "I am so glad you came and I'm glad I got to meet you." My heart sank as I watched Jay running all over the place screaming, laughing and crying all at once. I just kept thinking to myself, *I was right there*. I had to remind myself of something my mother would say. "When it's your time, nothing and nobody can stop you." For that minute, in that moment, it was Jay's time. Oprah had called his name and invited him to lunch. He was having his time — I would have mine. Folks around me kept saying, "Aren't you upset?" "That could have been you!" "You took him there and he got to meet Oprah." I had to stop listening to the negative whispers in my ear. I was trying to listen to what this extraordinary woman had to say.

At the beginning of the event Oprah was telling the audience, "Please don't ask me for autographs or ask to have a picture taken with me." She pointed out a lady in one of the front rows and said, "You asked me for my autograph yesterday while I was on the treadmill and what did I say to you?"

"You said no," she replied.

"That's because we were there to work out," Oprah said. "We weren't there to do meet and greets, and I wasn't there to take pictures. I had a great time talking with you, though. Didn't we have a great conversation?"

"Yes, we had a great time!" the lady replied. While this conversation was going on, I was trying to get refocused so I could listen to the important words Oprah would have to say.

She began to give her presentation, and listening to her impacted my heart even more than the first time I had seen her in Michigan. She was sharing lessons from her childhood, her hardships and her successes. I realized, once again, that we really had come from the same place. She was speaking of having a higher purpose in life, a higher calling. As a preacher's kid, I had heard that all my life. Oprah continued on, urging the crowd to think about what the voice of God was telling us to do. My father had always told us that. Get someplace quiet and listen to the voice of God. And I realized, at that moment, that I had been running through life not truly listening to what God had to tell me — all I had been doing was asking Him for things.

Everything Oprah was telling me, as I got really quiet and began to listen closely to what she had to say, spoke to my soul. I cried that day, for two hours. It was one of those ugly, sputtering, soul-wrenching cries. And then she said something that profoundly impacted me. "I don't believe in coincidence," she said. "You call people into your life based upon your intentions." She was speaking at that moment about how she got the role in *The Color Purple*, but she might as well have been talking about my life. And then Oprah began to quote the words to a song my mother would sing. It was an old spiritual song called "I Surrender All."

"I surrender all, all to thee my blessed Savior, I surrender all." All of these things she was saying, the song she was quoting, I had heard them all before from one person or another. My parents, Oprah, and many people had spoken these words. But at that moment, the culmination of all of these things truly impacted me. It seemed as though, for the first time, I truly understood. If you find yourself in a position of not knowing what you want or which direction you should be headed, take the time to sit back and reflect over your life. Examine the events to better understand the underlying meaning or lesson behind them. Use those experiences to better understand who you are. Then, work your way toward being the person that you want to be. Oprah said it best when she said, "God has a bigger dream for you than you could ever dream for yourself." She talked about how she had always dreamed of having twelve trees in front of her house, and when she was finally able to buy her house in California, she looked out the window and saw those twelve trees standing proud and tall. But when she took a moment to look past those twelve, she saw thousands of trees. And that's what God had intended in his dreams for her; to give her more than she could have ever imagined for herself.

As Oprah continued to speak to those in attendance, she would point to people in the crowd and allow them to ask questions. At one point she mentioned she had been in Texas and that's where she had met Dr. Phil. That's also where she had been sued. There was a lady behind me that tapped me on the shoulder and asked, "Didn't you say you were from Texas? You're never going to get to Oprah now!" People around her began to echo her sentiments, and once again I was surrounded by these negative whispers.

Oprah took a break for lunch, and I raced off to find Jay. I begged him, "Please! Take me with you to lunch!" But before Jay could even respond, the security guard jumped in and said, "No. Oprah said just Jay." *Crap*, I thought, *I'm not going to make it.* So I asked Jay if he could take a copy of the first article I ever wrote and get it signed by Oprah. Jay grabbed it and ran off ecstatic because he was going to have lunch with Oprah! Jay returned after lunch and handed me back the article, saying, "Cheryl, I almost didn't get this signed." I looked at my first article, "The Plain Truth," and saw that signature scrawled in blue permanent ink across the words. I clutched that article to my chest, held onto it for dear life, and cried. I went back to my seat at the end of the break and listened to the second half of what Oprah had to say. She was saying to listen to the voices, the positive whispers, in your life and ignore the negative ones.

The positive whispers were the voice of God and those were the ones you needed to really hear.

Oprah announced that she had some time to take just a few more questions. I kept raising my hand like a little kid at the back of the classroom, waving emphatically to get the teacher's attention. I was desperate at this point because I knew Oprah was going to leave the stage at any moment, and I feared that I wouldn't get my chance to talk with her. Oprah said she had time for one more question and I almost jumped out of my seat because I knew I had to get her attention. It must have worked, because she looked at me and said, "You." There was a moment of silence and I spoke up. "Oprah, I know you said not to ask you for anything," I said. "But, will you think about it and pray about it? I'd like for you to grant me an interview." This was my time! "I can validate everything you are telling these women here today. I got somewhere, got by myself, listened to the voices, and a voice told me I would be a writer. Regardless of those who told me I wasn't a writer and would never be a writer, I now have my own column." I held up the article and said, "You've already seen the column. Jay brought it to you. And I would be honored and thrilled if you would give me the opportunity to interview you." There was a collective gasp and then silence fell over the crowd as everyone waited in anticipation for her response. I had done exactly what we were told not to do. I had asked Oprah for something.

Oprah looked at me and said, "You know what? I'm going to grant your request. You've got your interview." That place went wild! People were clapping, cheering, patting me on the back, and some even hugged me. I had done it. I was getting my interview.

When I finally got my feet to move, I panicked and ran into the bathroom. What was I going to ask her? We hadn't been allowed to really bring anything in, so all I had was my purse. I dug through that purse like I was looking for buried treasure and managed to come up with a pen and a small journal. I headed out of the bathroom, not sure where I was supposed to go next. That's when Gayle King, Oprah's best friend, walked up and grabbed my arm. "I know it's crazy out here right now," she said. "Just hold on to me." As we maneuvered our way through the crowd, Gayle asked me, "Do you know what you've done? Do you know what you've landed?" Oh, I knew all too well what I had done. I could hardly believe it myself. There had been people from the local news stations I had talked to that week who said they couldn't get interviews because Oprah wasn't granting any. How had I managed? I had been living my life with a purpose, that's how. I had set my goals, just like Oprah had said that day on her show. I had been determined I would succeed. I had written down my goals and figured out how I was going to achieve them. I had purposed to go interview Oprah, and to place that article in the newspaper.

Gayle came with me to return to my seat and sat next to me as Oprah finished her final words to the audience. I was crying as I watched the stagehands bring up two chairs to prepare for the interview and beautiful flowers as if I was already ordained to be there. Oprah stepped off the stage with her arms outstretched toward me like she was my big sister. As we hugged, I cried some more. She said, "Okay, girl, get yourself together and ask me anything." We sat down across from each other in those beautiful chairs. I continued to cry, but still managed to ask my questions. As I asked a question, I'd wipe away tears as she answered. Gayle brought me a box of tissues, and I continued to wipe away the tears of joy as Oprah continued to answer my questions. At the end of the interview, she also signed my t-shirt that said "Oprah's #1 Fan." It was the culmination of everything I had planned for. I had gotten my interview, and Oprah had signed off on my efforts by signing both my newspaper article and my t-shirt — she had endorsed that I was indeed her number one fan.

When I walked away from that place that day, I was completely blown away and a little in shock. As I left, there was a gathering of about 75 to 100 Oprah fans waiting, asking me to sign their copy of Oprah's magazine. When I looked puzzled, one lady spoke up and said, "I want this because you're going to be somebody someday and I want to be able to tell people I met you here." When I got back home to Texas, I was looking over the Oprah website and the events surrounding the Florida appearance were noted in the community section. There were many comments from fans about what had happened with me at the end of the day, but one stood out to me. A lady wrote, "Cheryl, I saw you and it reminded me of Oprah when she was in *The Color Purple* with her sister. I tried to get the photographer over to take a picture of you because your silhouette together reminded me of the scene in the movie where they were clapping hands singing, 'You and me will never part,' and I wanted you to have a picture of that moment." She couldn't get the photographer over, but it was still nice to read and see the impact that moment had on someone else.

Oprah had asked that I send her a copy of the article once it was complete, and I did just that. A few weeks later I received an envelope from HARPO. When I opened it there was a white card with a green "O" from the desk of Oprah Winfrey. The message read, "Cheryl, I got your article. Good job." And it was signed, "Oprah!"

I have the audacity to believe that peoples everywhere can have three meals a day for their bodies, education and culture of their minds, and dignity, equality, and freedom for their spirits. I believe that what self-centered men have torn down, men other-centered can build up I still believe that one day mankind will bow before the altars of God and be crowned triumphant over war and bloodshed, and nonviolent redemptive goodwill will proclaim the rule of the land. - Martin Luther King Jr.

The destruction of Minnie's Food Pantry on Christmas Eve, 2009.

The angels who brought Minnie's to life.

Kevin Crawford of Wal-Mart, helping us get The Giving Movement off the ground.

Sharing a laugh with my dear friend, Erica Simon.

With my friends, Christie Jackson, Erica Simon and Danielle Roberts.

My first column, signed by Oprah Winfrey.

With the one-and-only Oprah Winfrey, 2003.

With Dr. Harry Cohen, who took a chance on me.

With Sarah Ferguson, the Duchess of York, 2002.

My radio show, "The Real Happy Hour," 2006.

Interviewing Will Smith, 2008.

With Zig Ziglar.

With Gayle King at Oprah's Live Your Best Life Weekend, May 2010.

With Cathie Black at Oprah's Live Your Best Life Weekend, May 2010.

With Dr. Oz at Oprah's Live Your Best Life Weekend, May 2010.

Michael Irvin, raising funds after the DayStar Deliverance Ministries roof collapsed, 1996.

With Emmitt Smith.

With Dallas Cowboys quarterback Troy Aikman, 1996.

With Miami Heat guard Dwyane Wade.

Getting a hug from basketball star and philanthropist Magic Johnson.

At a speaking engagement with Deion Sanders, 2009.

With Torii and Katrina Hunter, who made Minnie's food and toy drive a success in 2009.

My grandmother, Helen Allen — the lady who taught us to give.

Lynette and me as little girls.

Artis and me on our wedding day.

Lynette and me, Sisters of Savings.

My beautiful sons, R.J. and Artis, Jr., as children.

The men in my life: Artis, Jr., Artis, and R.J.

With my mother and role model, Minnie Hawthorne Ewing.

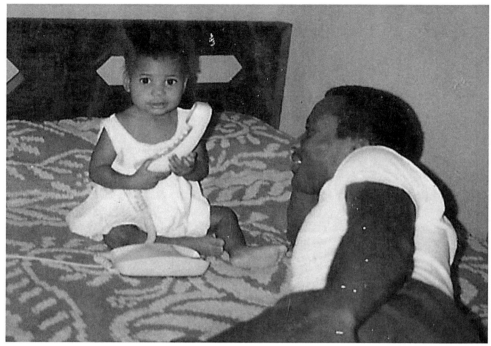

I was always a daddy's girl — my father never let my feet hit the floor.

My father, Robert Hawthorne, unsung hero.

Robert Hawthorne, Unsung Hero

Found me a home in glory, yes I did – John P. Kee, "I Bow Out"

My father was an awesome, powerful man of God. He never met a stranger and had a priceless smile that would light up a room. He was a Marine who had served his country with honor. He was a pastor, a lover of life, and a confidant. He was giving in every sense of the word and an amazing man, even if you weren't looking at him through the marveling eyes of a daddy's girl. He was a father to everyone who knew him and I wasn't the only one who called him "Papa." He gave the best bear hugs, hugs that instilled confidence in you that you were going to be okay, even when you felt like your world was caving in.

My father and I were very close, even from the moment I was born. I often look at early photos of him just staring at me sitting on the bed. I can see his side profile and he had such a proud grin on his face as he looked at me. He gave me any opportunity I asked for — but even more profound was that he believed in me. He thought I could do anything, and because of that, he refused to let me underachieve. I couldn't imagine life without him.

When my dad was eventually called into ministry it consumed not only his life, but also the life of our entire family. One year, we attended church all 365 days of the year. Oh, how I got tired of being in church. I would watch my father up there preaching and try to stay focused, but could only think about how badly I wanted to leave. Being a pastor isn't just a nine-to-five job. A pastor and his wife are there for the congregation at all times, day or night, seven days a week. We would be at home in the evening and the phone would ring and I would immediately get angry because I just knew it was someone from the church. This was my time to spend with my dad, and yet someone else in the congregation needed him more. That was a lot for a young girl to understand, and I would get insanely jealous of the interruptions. But my father was totally dedicated to God, his congregation and all of us. It wasn't until I was older that I realized just how dedicated he was and how hard he had to work to balance all those parts of his life. I understood then that my father was a true man of wisdom, and those people who would call him in their time of need truly did need him more than I at that moment.

Despite the fact that I felt like I needed to rebel against his lifestyle, I still loved my dad with all my heart and admired him above all. My husband had a lot to live up to when I left my parents' house to marry him at seventeen. And as my marriage progressed, there were times when I needed to lean on my dad's broad shoulders not only as my father, but also as my pastor. I was selective in what and how much I would share with him and my mom, only because I knew firsthand how much they already did for the congregation. I didn't want to burden them even further but they were always there to support my family and me. I often wondered if my dad knew how much I cared for him. Artis had known for a long time how much I loved and admired my father, and that was part of the reason he made the decision to buy that house across the street from my parents. We still live in that house to this day, and it has been a source of many very happy memories. It's also been a reminder of one of the saddest times in my life.

During the Christmas holidays in 2003, my father became ill. It started after my mom had suffered with a bad cold, and we assumed that's what my dad had. But after battling the "cold" for a week or so, he continued to get weaker and weaker and eventually ended up in the hospital. After running a gamut of tests that ruled out the flu and several other maladies, the doctors couldn't pinpoint exactly what was wrong. Dad began to feel better and was released. But a short time later, he became ill again and had to go back to the hospital. This happened time and again. Often, he would be so incoherent from illness that he couldn't even recognize us. In

February, the day before Valentine's Day and just over a month after he had gotten sick the first time, we were gathered at Dad's bedside and my heart was just breaking for my Mom. Here she was, standing at the bedside of the love of her life and he didn't even recognize who she was. He wasn't responding, not even to my mom's voice, and was almost comatose. We all left that day feeling crushed and defeated. We just didn't understand why this was all happening and so suddenly.

I woke up the next morning and immediately decided to go visit my dad. I walked in that Valentine's morning and found him alert, almost cheerful.
He looked at me and said, "How ya' doing' Miss Cheryl?"
I couldn't believe it. "Dad!" I yelled. After hugging him for a moment I asked him if he knew what day it was.
"No," he answered.
"It's Valentine's Day," I said. "Would you like me to call Mom for you?"
Of course he did, and I put the phone to his ear once Mom had answered and he said, "Happy Valentine's Day, Sweetheart." Of course my mom immediately dropped the phone, got dressed and moved at the speed of light to be at my dad's side. I stood and watched as they connected with each other just as they always had. It was truly miraculous. Dad recovered over the next week and was sent home yet again. My father was a lover of gospel music, and one of his favorite groups was the Bolton Brothers. He used to pull up in front of the house, stop, and scream for me to come outside just so I could hear the singing and the preaching of Pastor L.W. Bolton. The words and the music were something that always put a smile on his face. Even though Dad had come home from the hospital, he was still very ill and bedridden, so I asked if he would like me to bring him some of his favorite gospel music to help pass the time. I thought that if he could connect with the music, it might help him to recover for good. Sure enough, the Bolton Brothers music was what my father responded to most during his times of illness. His eyes lit up and his lips stretched into a smile of contentment at listening to those southern gospel songs. I immediately decided if that was what my dad responded to, then I was going to do everything in my power to be sure he had some contact with

his favorite group. I went home that day, looked up the name of the Bolton's publicist on the computer, and got ready to start placing as many phone calls as it would take.

Amazingly, their publicist answered the phone himself the first time I called. I could hardly contain myself as I began to explain how much of an impact the Bolton's had made on my father's life. I sobbed as I told of my dad's illness, his reaction to the music I brought to him and how desperate we were to have him healed. Of course, I had been praying and praying that my father would recover; after all, my parents had always taught us the power of prayer. So it was out of sheer desperation that I had placed this call and hoped if I could have one of the brothers even just call my dad that he would respond with a resounding recovery. Maybe the combination of prayer and music would heal him. I was desperate. I had to try.

The publicist put me in touch with James Bolton and I asked him if I could call him directly when I got over to my dad's house. He said he'd be happy to talk with my dad so I ran across the street, got on the phone, dialed up James Bolton and handed the phone to my father. Once Dad realized who he was speaking to, his eyes lit up and he got very animated. I stood watching my dad speaking more clearly than he had in two months and thought for sure this was the miracle we had all been waiting for. James was telling my dad to be sure to take care of his body because it was a temple, and I just cried watching my father respond to that simple phone call. James not only talked with my dad that day, but also continued to contact him over the next several months, checking in on his condition and reminding him to take care of himself. The Bolton family as a whole took our family under their wing during my dad's illness. It's amazing how perfect strangers can mean so much to you in your time of need. I was so sure that my prayers, my dad's music and the support from the Bolton family would push my father into a permanent recovery.

But, once again, Dad ended up back in the hospital and it was becoming apparent that something was really wrong with him. The doctors still couldn't figure it out and, while they continued to run tests, his condition continued to bounce up and down. One day when he seemed to be doing particularly well I asked him, "Dad, are you going to be okay?"

He answered, "Everything's going to be all right." That was his mantra to us during his times of illness. So, it didn't strike me as odd when I was leaving and he called me back into the room. "Cheryl," he said, "take care of your mom for me."

"Okay, Dad," I responded and left the room to catch up with my mom. But I suddenly turned and ran back into his room and asked, "You mean to take care of mom until you get out of the hospital, right?"

My father simply responded, "Everything's going to be all right."

My father was growing increasingly ill. The doctors told us he was in acute renal failure, but still hadn't identified the cause of the illness. He was having a difficult time keeping any food or fluids down and didn't have an appetite anyway. His legs and feet were swelling and he had almost constant pain in his back and side. They began to give him dialysis several times a week, but my dad was beginning to lose his faculties and hardly understood what was happening. He was restless and confused. In fact, Dad was at the point where he didn't really recognize any of us and it was heartbreaking. This man, my father, the strongest man I knew, was suddenly so weak. It had been less than six months since he first came down with that cold or flu or whatever it was, and now he lay in a hospital bed, a shell of what he was, and almost totally helpless. I would often just sit and look at him, remembering all the good times, not understanding why this was happening, and crying so hard I thought I would collapse there in the bed next to him. Often times I wanted to.

I have said my father was a true man of God. That was even more apparent in those days. As he would slip in and out of being coherent, he would speak to each one of us in turn, asking if we were ready for the challenge, ready to be strong. Every other word he spoke during those times of clarity was of the Lord. When I worked for Emmitt Smith, I would bring my dad autographed footballs from the different Cowboys players I had met. I thought this would make him happy because he was such a fan. He was always appreciative, but never got overly excited about those mementos. But one unexpected moment had brought tears to his eyes. He was in the pulpit one Sunday and asked if someone would volunteer to read a scripture passage to the congregation. When I picked up my Bible and volunteered to read, my father couldn't have been prouder. He smiled as tears glistened in his eyes. Of all the things I had given him, the greatest gift had been to demonstrate my love for God to the congregation of his church. That's what made a man of God truly happy.

My father eventually became so ill that the hospital didn't feel there was anything further they could do for him and told us to take him home. They made arrangements for a hospice nurse to come to check on him. That's when I knew they were sending my dad home to die. It was heart wrenching. I couldn't help but hope that my prayers would still be answered, but deep in my heart I knew we were losing him. We all gathered at my father's bedside, each taking turns lying with him and sobbing and telling him how much we loved him. He didn't know we were there, and that made it even more difficult. We had to be sure that this man — our strength, our confidante, our preacher and our dad — understood how much we loved him and how desperate we were not to lose him. We were screaming his name and our tears were drenching his face, but we just couldn't get a response from him. It took the prayers of a little boy to bring Dad to consciousness just one last time.

My nephew, Charles, was only five years old during my father's illness, and my dad just loved that little boy. He had given him the nickname Sir Charles; they were buddies and just enjoyed each other's company and all the activities a grandfather and grandson enjoy. As we were gathered at my father's bedside, sweet little Charles went up to the bed and quietly asked, "May I pray for Papa?" All at once my dad opened his eyes and he lay there listening as Charles softly prayed that God would heal his Papa.

The power of prayer from a little boy had brought my father back to us just one last time.

I sat at my father's bedside reading the Bible and praying to God that if he was going to raise him up, then raise him up and heal him. I didn't want him to continue to be in the state he was in. Dad's breathing was becoming increasingly labored and there began to be long pauses between each breath. Five seconds, ten seconds, longer. I sat and listened as he took each ragged breath, hoping and praying it wasn't his last. Artis and I decided to stay at my mother's house across the room from where my father laid. It was difficult. His breathing rattled so loudly, we could hear it above the hum of the ceiling fan. It seemed like my heart stopped beating each time I would hear the pause in his breathing.

Hospice sent a nurse to the house, and when she entered she announced that they called her the Angel of Death. When I asked her why she said, "Because every patient I've been sent to care for has died."
I asked her, "My father's going to die, isn't he?"
She asked if I really wanted to know the answer to that question. When I told her I did, she replied, "Yes, he's going to die."

I knew in my gut it was coming, but I hadn't wanted to admit it. I had been blindly faithful that my prayers would be answered, that the Lord would heal my father and bring him back to us. But the signs were all there and now this nurse was confirming my darkest fears. She and I discussed his symptoms and reality set in. My dad was already gone. It was only a shell lying there in that bed. However, I still held on to faith. That's what this man of God had taught me. I rested in God's ability to raise the dead, heal the sick and perform miracles, even in the 21st century.

Artis and I stayed that first night and Dad made it through. I was relieved. We didn't want to chance even having to cross the street to be at Dad's side if and when the Lord called him home. On the afternoon of Friday,

June 18, I was in the bathroom of my parents' home, spending extra time on my hair. Usually, I was lazy and only curled the front of my hair, but my dad always liked it when I curled it all the way around to the back. So that's what I did. I knew my dad was beyond the point of seeing me, but I still wanted to look good for him. I was listening to music as I curled my hair — a song by John P. Kee. The lyrics were powerful:

I bow out gracefully
After all that you have done
Gracefully
You are my morning sun
Gracefully
As I leave I bow out gracefully

I bow out gratefully
A few enemies I still have
Gratefully
Every void in my life, You are there
All I want to say is
Gratefully
As I leave, I bow out

I'm grateful
I'm moving gracefully
Gently with form
Meek and humble
I've got to go

Found me a home in glory, yes I did

As he sang the words, "Found me a home in glory," Artis knocked on the door. When I opened it, my husband uttered the worst words I had heard in my life. "Your dad's gone." The man who had held my hand when I was a little girl had taken his final breath holding my husband's hand.

Robert C. Hawthorne was called home to God at 1:09 p.m. on June 18, 2004, and I still can't believe it. Have you ever loved someone so much that you thought you could not live without them? My father was gone. He would never be able to see the things he had prayed his little girl would be or become.

My heart was beyond broken. The pain was so intense I might as well have been shot, or hit by a bus, or both. There weren't words to describe the way I was feeling. My journal entry from that day was simple:

Dad died today. Is my life over, too? I have no drive. I can't eat or sleep and tears are flowing. The God I love so much took my father and friend. I am angry. I am so confused. Dad was incredible. He was soft- spoken. He was a man of honor and I miss him already.

Several weeks later, the entry reads:

Every Friday it's worse. I cry and cry. At 1:09 p.m. I always look at a clock and the tears begin to fall. Lord, help me help myself. Mom said I'm going to grieve to death. Who cares? I'd be with my dad. I see no reason to live.

Those thoughts were real, and they continued to be real for almost a year after losing my dad. At 1:09 p.m. each Friday, something would come over me. Something so powerful I couldn't shake it. Nobody could help me get through it, nobody but God.

There are things that will happen to you in your life that you won't be able to avoid. Things that will be painful, experiences will happen that make you hurt beyond what you thought was possible. Things that will make you feel like you just can't go on. But you have to make your way through them. I learned that, even as my father was going through his illness. You have to push your way through. I pushed my way through, helping plan my dad's funeral. As a token of his love, my mother gave my dad's praying hands charm to me so I would know he was always watching over me. I needed that.

Since Dad was a Marine, we asked the funeral director about military honors but were told they couldn't do it. We continued to plan the services, and on the day of the funeral, the limo picked us up to take us to the church. The outpouring of support was overwhelming. So many people got up to speak, and the majority of them referred to my dad as "Papa." My mother was strong beyond words. I will never know how she found the strength to preach my father's eulogy. She held her head high as she gave her sermon, titled "You are going to die." The love in the room was palpable.

Unbeknownst to us, the limo driver was a bugler for military funeral honors and an instructor for the local Reserve Officer Training Corps. When he saw the number of people attending the funeral, heard the stories of love and life about my dad, and then realized he was a former Marine, the driver jumped into action. When we arrived at the graveside, there were the cadets from the ROTC program ready to perform the flag folding ceremony. Then the driver pulled out his bugle and reverently played "Taps" for my dad. It was one final thing that told everyone what a great and honorable man my father was. I miss him to this day.

Ten or fifteen years from now, which is not that far away, someone you love will die. I urge you to tell them all the words right now that I wish I could tell my father just one more time. Celebrate your heroes and then become one. Don't let any moment pass you by.

There Are No Coincidences

Sometimes you really can't listen to what anybody else says. You just gotta listen inside. You're not supposed to end up in those mines. You know why? 'Cause I think you made other plans. – Miss Riley, "October Sky"

Before my father's condition had become grave, I'd walked into his hospital room to find him watching "The Oprah Winfrey Show." Dad knew what a fan I was, and as we watched together, I recalled that Oprah's staff had posted to her website that they were producing a show around the theme of dying wishes. At the time, none of us had any idea that my dad was truly dying, but he was enthusiastic about making a video from his hospital bed asking Oprah to send his daughter to a taping of her show. Looking back, making that video was a sign that Dad knew what was to come, but nobody understood it at the time. In the video, he smiled that famous smile of his and told Oprah why I needed to be at her show. At the end, I turned the camera on myself and said, "Oprah, when I come to your show, I want to interview you and my favorite actress, Julia Roberts."

Of course, the realization that my father was indeed on his deathbed came quickly, and in our family's grief and helplessness, I misplaced the tape. After my father passed away, the next three months went by in a daze, and all I remembered about the video was the fun we'd had making it. It was one of the last happy moments we'd shared — one I will treasure forever. I had completely forgotten that the tape had never been sent.

But my wish came true anyway. I got tickets to her show! I was going to see Oprah. For the first time in months, my grief over the loss of my father lifted, and I allowed myself to be excited. So before we left for Chicago, I came up with a little song to the tune of *YMCA*.

Oprah!
I'm your number one fan, I said
Oprah!

Nobody else in the land, I said
Oprah!
Thanks for all that you do and we love you, love you, love you
Stedman!
Please say my name every day, and
Gayle!
Don't let my name slip away
My friends and family
Wanted to be here with me but they're watching me on their TV
Hey, Hey, Hey, Hey!
It's fun to be on O-P-R-A-H!
It's fun to be on O-P-R-A-H!

You get the idea. I was just so excited to be going, and the song was a way to express my happiness.

My girlfriend Erica and I headed to Chicago for the taping, and the morning of the show, I was sitting in the middle of the bed in the hotel room just daydreaming. Erica looked at me thoughtfully and asked, "What are you thinking, Cheryl?"

I smiled a little sheepishly and replied, "You know, I was thinking I am like Oprah. I may not have millions of dollars or a TV show, but I've got a heart like hers. I can see myself having my own show, doing exactly what she's doing." Erica said she could see it, too. I was touched, just as I'm always touched when people believe in me. But I am even more touched when someone close to me believes. It is powerful to have a friend — someone who knows your worst flaws — appreciate you for who you truly are.

We were two of the first in line to enter Oprah's studio that day, but the last to be seated. I just knew we were going to end up in the back of the studio audience because of it. That was disappointing to me because I had waited so long to get here, but fate stepped in once again. I got seated on the front row, corner seat, and right against the aisle where Oprah enters.

Erica was seated in the row right behind me. We were so excited! We were screaming and yelling, making sure everyone knew just how happy we were to be there. As we waited for the show to begin, the stage crew indicated they were having technical difficulties and would get the show underway as quickly as possible. So the audience handler asked us, "While we wait, does anyone have a poem they could do or anything they want to say?"

Well hellooooo! I cried out, "I've got a song! I'll sing it!" So I got up and began to sing my Oprah song. The audience loved it. Of course, the song only took a minute or so to sing, and they were still having technical issues. A few minutes later, the same gentleman came back out and said, " We liked your song, Cheryl." And suddenly, I heard the melody to *YMCA* bursting out of the speakers into the audience. Before I knew what was happening, I was pulled back up on stage and was belting out my song along with the background music. Of course, you can't sing anything that sounds like *YMCA* without dancing as well — and nobody loves to dance like I do! It was a blast. I entertained the audience while the crew tried to work out their malfunctions.

After I had gone back to my seat, the handler asked the audience, "How many of you like Cheryl?" The audience members clapped and cheered enthusiastically. He asked me where I was from, and I proudly replied that I was Texas born and bred. He said, "Okay, Cheryl, we're going to warm up this crowd." And he looked at the audience and said, "What we want you to do is pretend that Cheryl is Oprah. Cheryl, come on back up here." I was in my element! I stepped up on stage across from where he was standing, and he said, "Cheryl, pretend you're Oprah." And I said, "Well then, you're in the wrong place. Oprah stands over there. And her guests are over here." He just laughed and said, "Oh, no. What I want you to do is go out those double doors and come back in like you're Oprah making her entrance. Audience, when she comes back in, we want you to scream and yell as if she's Oprah." I started sniffling right then and there, and the audience coordinator said, "Oprah doesn't cry!"

And I looked at him and said, "Well, I'm not really Oprah." But I was going to give it a shot.

I marched down that aisle and I walked out the double doors. Then, I turned around and faced the doors, took a deep breath, and exploded through them down the "I love you" tunnel. It's the aisle Oprah walks down as she enters the show, and everyone's screaming and yelling, "I love you!" And they were doing the same for me at that moment. One woman jumped out into the middle of the aisle and gave me this great big bear hug, just like my father used to.

The audience was still yelling and screaming at me as I marched up to the stage, waving to everyone as I sat down. And then I jumped right back up again realizing I was sitting where the guests sit. If I was Oprah, I had to sit in Oprah's seat! For that moment, I really was Oprah. The audience members laughed and cheered, and then it was time for the real Oprah to come to the stage. So I headed back to my seat along the aisle to wait for the real talk show queen to come out. As Oprah entered the studio, and everyone yelled and screamed, she got to the stage and said, "Wow! What is going on out here? What happened?" Everyone just yelled, "It's Cheryl!" as they pointed at me. Oprah looked at me and said, "What happened?" I replied, "It's not me, it's you! They're excited to see you." Oprah proceeded to tell us what a great show she had for us that day. "I'm here ... and Julia Roberts is here!"

I almost fell over from shock. All at once the realization slapped me in the face and I knew my father had a hand in this moment. I had said on that videotape in his hospital room that I wanted to interview Oprah and my favorite actress, Julia Roberts. At that instant I realized they must have gotten my dad's dying wish tape, and I was going to interview Oprah and Julia Roberts. I could hardly pay attention during the show because I knew I wasn't prepared for these interviews. I had to think of what I was going to ask, and the butterflies kept racing in my stomach the whole time.

We went through the hour of the show and Julia Roberts left the stage. The coordinator told Oprah, "We have to bring Cheryl up. She has a song for you." So they brought me up and I sang my song once again as I watched Oprah dance along with my song. Then Oprah excused herself and left the stage. I looked at the coordinator and asked him, "Is she coming back?" He clearly didn't understand what I meant. So I asked him again, "Is she coming back?"

He answered, "What do you mean is she coming back?"

I said, "My dad's dying wish. My wildest dream to interview Oprah and Julia Roberts. You got the tape. Is she coming back?"

He said, "I'm sorry, we didn't get a tape."

They didn't get the tape? Then how was I there on the day Julia Roberts had given her only interview while pregnant with her twins? Suddenly, I remembered: in the trauma of my dad's illness and death, I had misplaced the tape. It had never even been sent. This was just a moment in time, a coincidence.

But, like Oprah says, nothing happens by coincidence, and what had happened that day was no coincidence. I was wearing my father's praying hands, given to me when he passed away, and I looked down at them and silently thanked my dad for a great time. I only wished he could have been there to hear this crazy story in person.

The Reminder

A year after my father passed away, I was finally starting to get back to the business of living. About that time, I heard that Fergie, the Duchess of York, was bringing her tour to Dallas. Since I'd first met her to have my mother's china signed, Fergie had lost weight with Weight Watchers and had written multiple books on weight loss and nutrition. She was now touring the country, promoting positive lifestyle changes and giving talks about health and nutrition. It was a positive message, but until I lost my father, I thought it didn't pertain to me. After his death, though, the message was suddenly very clear. She insisted that sometimes people need help getting healthy, and that you have to be adamant, for their own sake, that they take their health seriously. I really felt that if I had done more to help my dad take care of himself, we wouldn't have lost him the way we did. I wanted to thank the Duchess for spreading her message, because she wasn't just helping people lose weight — she was saving lives.

I found the picture I'd taken with the Duchess years earlier, and had it framed and engraved. I wanted to give it to her to make sure she knew that her message was being heard and that she was touching hearts. Sometimes people get discouraged and need help remembering that their work is not in vain. I wanted to give her that reminder. Of course, I managed to sit in the front row of her speaking engagement, and during her speech, tears were streaming down my face as I thought about my father and how he might have still been alive if only he'd taken better care of himself. She noticed me crying, and, after she spoke, asked to meet with me. I poured out my heart, telling her how powerful her message was to me, and thanking her. Then, I gave her the engraved photo.

She looked at the picture, and then back up at me, and asked, "Do you know who you are?"

"No," I replied.

"You are my Oprah."

My eyes filled with tears once again. I'd never received such a compliment in my life. I was just a plain ol' girl from Dallas, Texas. Cheryl Jackson was the Duchess of York's Oprah? I didn't know what to say.

Sarah and I talked for another half hour, and then she made me a proposal. She was going to continue to work in the U.S. and needed a staff. "I am adopting families in New York, and I need someone to be my liaison," she said. "I need a caring person who can keep track of them and give me information about their lives, like birthdays, anniversaries and such. I want to be able to send them cards and gifts when appropriate." She thought I would be the perfect person to do this for her. I was ecstatic. She would fly me back and forth from Texas to New York to perform these tasks. I agreed in a heartbeat!

Unfortunately, weeks later, Sarah's publicist called and said they had recommended to her that they hire someone in New York to do the job. I was disappointed, but I understood their logic. I will always love Fergie, and hope to have another chance to work with her someday.

Faith, and the Game of Life

By this time, my experience had taught me that there was no limit to the things a plain ol' girl from Dallas, Texas, could accomplish. Enough crazy coincidences had happened that I was a full-fledged believer in the power of God, the power of prayer, the power of faith … and the power of hard work and persistence. So when I found out about the first season of the "Deal or No Deal" show, I jumped on the opportunity. I already had game show experience — I had done poorly in "Scrabble" and then even worse at celebrity "Wheel of Fortune" (with former Dallas Cowboy Bill Bates). My sister had almost won the showcase showdown in "The Price is Right," too, so my family and I felt that we were long overdue for a win.

I had no idea what the premise of "Deal or No Deal" was. All I knew was that you had the chance to win a million dollars. There were already a lot of game shows on at the time, and the one that stuck out in my mind was "Fear Factor." You know, the one where you have to eat the bugs and jump off of buildings to win $50,000? Um, no! I would never subject myself to those kinds of stunts. All I saw about "Deal or No Deal" was that it was hosted by Howie Mandell and somehow involved opening suitcases. That was much more my speed. I told my family, "I am going to be on that show!" Once again, if you want something to happen you have to say it. Dream it, speak it and will it into reality. So I went online to find out what it would take to become a contestant. What I found was that you had to send in an audition tape to the producers. Unfortunately, I had no idea where or who to send the videotape to, so I said a prayer, Googled the words "deal or no deal," and found eight addresses. I randomly put names that I saw on the Internet with addresses and hoped that I would get to at least one person. I knew in order to get their attention, my video needed to be unique, but I was a bit starved for ideas on what to do.

Our church had just moved into a new building, and the place was basically empty. No pews, no computers for the staff, nothing. Being a preacher's kid, I knew I had to do something to help the church and to help friends and family who were struggling. I realized that winning big on "Deal or No Deal" would be just the solution we needed. One Sunday after church was over, I grabbed my sister Lynette, asked her to turn on the video camera, and as soon as she hit the button I said, "Hi, this is Cheryl Jackson. Look no further, I am your next contestant." I gave them the reasons behind why I needed to be a contestant, telling them all about the church and the needs of my family and friends. I had read on the website that contestants were allowed to bring along four supporters to California. As usual, I wasn't going to get this opportunity and not try to help someone else in the process. My brother, Darius, happened to be a songwriter and musician who had always wanted to write a jingle. Most of our choir members had never been out of the state of Texas, much less on a plane. So I said on the tape that if I was selected, I wanted them to allow my brother to write a jingle and allow the entire 36-member choir to come with me. I knew that was very bold — maybe even crazy — but I had to ask.

I immediately sent the tape off to the producers. They received the video on a Monday, and on Tuesday night, Lynette called me and said, "Okay, so you're not gonna tell me?" "Tell you what?" I asked. "You're not gonna tell me!" she exclaimed. I had no idea what she was talking about. When I had filled out the application for the show, I had put Lynette down as my alternate contact person. I hadn't checked my voicemails yet, so when Lynette said, "I got the call, too," I still had no clue what she was talking about. "I got the call, too!" she insisted. "So, if you want to play this game, I'll play the game with you." I just kept laughing because I still had no inkling of what she was referring to. We went round and round like that until I finally said, "Lynette, what in the world are you talking about?" She shouted, "They called me! They called me!" I was finally screaming into the phone, "Who? Who called you?"

"You really don't know?" she said. Of course I didn't, so she shouted, "Deal or No Deal!" They're trying to reach you!" I went nuts again as she told me to check my voicemail. Sure enough, they had. It was late that night so when I returned the phone call nobody was in the office and I had to wait until the next day to talk to someone. That felt like the longest night of my life. I was so excited I could hardly contain myself. The wait was agonizing.

The next day, they hadn't called yet, so Artis and I headed out to the movies. I left my cell phone on during the movie just in case. Sure enough, I got a call from John, the contestant coordinator, during the middle of the film. He said they had received my tape and wanted to talk to me. Normally, I would have to go to a city where they were doing a contestant search, but this time they were sending someone out to us. I couldn't believe my luck!

On the scheduled date, my husband, friends and I met the contestant coordinator at the American Airlines Admiral's Club at the airport. I was already feeling fancy just going into the Admiral's Club (I hadn't even known it existed). I knew this game was about choosing a suitcase and I had decided I would choose case number three. This would be the third time I would be on a game show. I had three wonderful men in my life: my husband and my two sons. I also had three fantastic girlfriends: Danielle, Erica and Christie. Being that my mother is a minister, the number three for the Holy Trinity was an obvious one: the Father, the Son and the Holy Spirit. Everything was leading me to that number three case. At the airport, we began to play a mock version of the game. Chandra was standing next to me as I played and I chose case number three. The game continued and I wasn't doing very well. We got down to the final three cases; the one I had chosen and two others. There were three amounts left on the board - $1,000, $10,000 and $100,000. When time came to choose another case, Chandra told me to pick case number nine. So I did and wouldn't you know that case held the $100,000? I played my case all the way to the end and when it was opened it held the $1,000. Everybody started laughing but it was okay. As we headed home, I reminded myself this was just a mock game and that when I made it to that stage as a contestant, case number three would have my million dollars.

About a week went by, and as we were sitting in church and at the end of service, my mother said, "We have an announcement to make." I was just as curious as the rest of the congregation. My mom continued, "Cheryl, we have a great message for you. You've been chosen for 'Deal or No Deal!'" The entire congregation began to rejoice and celebrate. When my mother finally managed to get everyone quieted down, she continued, "I have another announcement. The entire choir will be going with her!" When I tell you the atmosphere in that church was astounding, it's an understatement. People were screaming, crying and running up and down the aisles. The feeling was absolutely amazing. I understood what Oprah must feel like when she's giving away gifts from her "Favorite Things" list, because I was able to give those choir members something they may have never been able to give to themselves. There is no feeling like it in the world.

We all waited in anticipation for the day we would fly to Los Angeles to tape the show. Hardly anybody could bear the suspense. I took my girlfriends out to dinner and asked for a deposit slip to their checking accounts. I was going to hook them up and show them my gratitude for standing by me. I even wrote checks out to my family members and my church. I could hardly contain myself leading up to the day of our departure. You should have seen this huge group of us getting on that plane, off to start our adventure. The atmosphere was perfect for what was about to happen. I could feel hope in the air. I was so happy that in a few days, all the people I loved would not have to worry about finances any longer.

The day of taping, my four on-stage supporters and I showed up at the studio at 7 a.m. to fill out stacks of paperwork and hear what the staff had to tell us about non-disclosures and all kinds of "legal stuff," as Chandra put it. We were escorted everywhere we went, even to the bathroom! Of course I had been on game shows before, but I still couldn't get over all the hustle and bustle of the crew, the hurried talking into headsets, the bright lights, and the excitement. As I was led out to the front of the audience section, I saw my supporters being led to their seats. I waved and tried to compose myself before the game began.

I had told myself I was going to pick case number three as my case for the game. I had even told the producers that backstage. Just before I went on stage, though, someone asked me what I would do if the number three suitcase did not have the million dollars in it. I froze suddenly, and when I got on the stage and Howie asked me to pick my suitcase number, I blurted out 16, the age of my youngest son. Wait, what had I just said? I had chosen case number sixteen instead of three! I don't know if it was the excitement or the bright lights or what, but the choice was made and I proceeded to play the game. I opened case after case that day, going back and forth from larger numbers to smaller amounts. I opened the first six cases, and was then offered $10,000 and rejected it. Five more cases, a $31,000 offer and "No Deal." At the end of the day, all the biggest amounts were still on the board, including the $1 million. I was set up for success the second day. We were all pumped leaving the studio, but we weren't allowed to tell the choir members what had happened during the first part of taping, because of the non-disclosure clauses and red tape.

The next day, we walked in again bright and early, waiting for my name to be called. As I finally headed out to the stage, they guided my supporters to their special couch in front of the stage. I could see our entire choir sitting in the audience, and they started to cheer and wave as I came out. It was just awesome. Howie Mandell introduced me and got everyone caught up on what had happened the day before. He introduced my supporters, and we were off and running again. I had to open four cases, and the first one I opened had the $500,000 in it. That was pretty harsh but

I was there to win the million, right? I opened small amounts on the next three cases and the banker offered me $48,000. Nope. "No Deal."

What happened next was devastating. I hadn't picked my number three case at the beginning of the show and decided now was the time to open it. I held my breath as the beautiful model slowly opened her case. I could tell as she peeked inside the amount was not good. When she dramatically revealed the amount, I just couldn't believe it. Case number three, MY case, had the million dollars in it. It felt like a gunshot to the heart. I opened two more cases; one with $50,000 and one with $500, and the banker offered me $39,000. I was tempted to take it after opening that one million dollar case, but there were still two big amounts left on the board. I still had the chance to win $300,000 or $750,000 … so "No Deal."

The next round I opened two more cases with smaller amounts in them and was offered $66,000. "No Deal." Once again Chandra yelled at me to open case number 19 and I did. The case revealed $750 and I got an offer of $97,000 from the banker. Both big amounts were still on the board, so "No Deal." I looked at my mom in the audience at the front of the choir group and thought she was going to faint, but I was going for it! The next case I chose was number five and the model revealed $200. The audience, the choir and my supporters were all going crazy. We waited for the banker to call and give me his offer. When Howie put down the phone he gave me the news, the offer was $172,000. That was more money than any of us had seen in our lives. I instantly felt overwhelmed. Chandra fell to the floor, banging her fists. I think my mom was in disbelief. After all the dramatics were over, everyone was shouting, "No Deal! No Deal!" I took a look at the board and realized the two big amounts were still there, and there were only four cases left: mine and three to eliminate. I could feel it in my bones. This was my day to help make dreams come true for my family, my friends and my church. So with all my might, I grabbed hold of the case covering the red Deal button, closed my eyes and shouted, "No Deal!" as I slammed the case shut. The audience went crazy. I thought I was going to faint. Howie let the choir sing the jingle Darius had written as we went into a commercial break, and gave me time to regain my composure.

I could hardly stand it. My heart was about to beat out of my chest. As we came back from break, I thought, *here we go.* I chose my next case, number 25. I held my breath as the case was opened and revealed $750,000. The audience was devastated. There were only three cases left, but the $300,000 was still in play. There was no way, after three game shows and all this drama that I was going home with just a few dollars. The call came in from the banker with his offer of $80,000. My husband, who had not said a word during the entire game, was asked by Howie what he thought I should do. He said "Cheryl, look at me." I stopped and looked as he shouted, "No Deal!" I had come this far and I wasn't turning back. I heard someone say, "She's from the South so she will listen to her husband." They were right. I yelled out, "No Deal!" and slammed the cover closed. One last case to choose, and I chose number 26. The audience and I collectively held our breath as the case was opened to reveal … $300,000. That was it, it was over. The banker offered me $2 and I quickly rejected it. "No Deal." Now I had to decide to either keep my case or trade for the other case. I had chosen my case and I was sticking with it. Howie opened my case to reveal what I had won: five dollars. I had the chance to walk away with $172,000 and I went home with $5. I told Howie that money didn't make me happy — the people who came with me made me happy. I walked away and passed by several of the models, who were crying because they had held the larger dollar amounts in their suitcases. I assured them that I would be okay.

I didn't financially help all the people that I had set out to bless. The checks that I had pre-written for them would not be cashed, neither would any big deposits be made. I was extremely disappointed in myself for letting them down. But, many of them had come along for the exciting ride and had an unforgettable experience. In the end, it was a great experience. I received my $5.00 check and I decided not to cash it. I photo copied it and mailed it back to them with the words, "NO DEAL" written in bold red ink. On the 100th episode, I received a call to see if I wanted to attend the taping. The call came just two days before the show was to be taped, and the airline tickets were over $1,000. I reminded them that I had only won $5.00 and I couldn't afford to pay for a ticket at that price. Looking back, I wish I had. During that show the contestant that had previously won the least amount had gotten a chance to play another game. If I had gone, that would have been me. I still read that email and realize that could have been another opportunity that got away.

After the show aired, I set up a website called "Match my Money" and asked people to help me continue my charity work by matching the five dollars that I had won on "Deal or No Deal." The first donation I received was from Dr. Harry Cohen for $500. I couldn't believe my eyes. What a blast from the past! I knew Dr. Cohen believed in me, and he continued to validate that. I hope our paths will cross again.

"Deal or No Deal" was another game show loss, but I was telling the truth when I said my friends and family meant more to me than money. What an experience for all of us! And what a lesson in following my instincts. I had planned to pick suitcase #3, but I let someone put doubt in my mind. Next time, that won't happen. Will there be a next time? I sure hope so! Like they say: if at first you don't succeed, try, try again.

Lessons on the Red Carpet

Each of us represents a star in heaven. Sometimes we shine with the rest, sometimes we twinkle alone, and sometimes, when we least expect it, we make someone's dreams come true. – Anonymous

Since I had grown up in a strict religious household and had never been allowed to wear makeup, it seemed a bit crazy that I wanted to be on TV. I was always told I couldn't do it because you had to wear makeup to be on camera. Like that was going to stop me. So when my best friend Erica told me Fox television was going to do a 16-city tour to find someone to help host their Oscar segment, she asked, "Are you going to go?" Of course I was going to go! I asked Erica to go with me on yet another adventure.

On the day the tour came to Dallas, we headed out to Grapevine Mills Mall along with about a thousand other people. Arthel Nevell was one of the hosts of Fox's "Good Day Live" at the time, and she was helping with the casting. Arthel had been the first African American on-air reporter at KVUE-TV in Austin, and I admired her quite a bit. I had to fill out a sheet telling the producers why I wanted to host the Oscar segment. I wrote down that I wanted to prove that a plain ol' girl from Dallas, Texas, who does not wear any makeup, pants, or jewelry can still be somebody. For our audition, we were to sit behind a desk next to Arthel, and act as if we were reading the teleprompter and hosting the show. Arthel and I bantered back and forth, exchanging dialogue, and I felt a rush of excitement. I just knew I was going to be chosen to host the Oscar segment. I was given a card by one of the producers and told they'd contact me if I was chosen.

Over the next two months, I waited on pins and needles to get that phone call from Fox. But when the weeks passed with no word, I couldn't contain myself anymore. I pulled out that business card, picked up the phone, and called to find out what was going on. The person on the other end of the phone told me someone had already been chosen. *Boy, was I off on that one*, I thought. I was so sure I was going to be chosen, and it was a real disappointment to find out otherwise.

But then, about six weeks later, I got a phone call from one of the executives at Fox. He told me they had narrowed down their search for an Oscar segment host to three people, and I was one of them! Just as I had when Adora Cox called and offered to finance our house, I almost dropped the phone. I had been under the impression they'd already selected someone, and I had put the whole thing out of my mind. I told the executive this, and he replied, "Well, I'm not sure who told you that but they were wrong. Are you still interested?" Of course I was! I guess the old saying is true: it ain't over 'til it's over. I was told they needed to know where I would be the day they announced their selection, because they were going to position live cameras outside the finalists' homes and announce the winner on air. I told them I would be at home watching the show.

The day of the show arrived, and my house was packed with family friends. We sat on the edges of our seats as "Good Day Live" began. Who would be selected? The segment began and the atmosphere of our home was absolutely electric. Who had they chosen? It seemed like the hosts took way too long to introduce the segment. We were on pins and needles. Finally, the hosts made the announcement. "We've chosen a winner to co-host our Oscar segment. Will you go to their door now, please?" You could see the camera start to walk up toward a house, and the camera was angled down so as not to spoil the surprise. But the sidewalk in front of our house has a very distinctive gravel look to it — and as soon as I saw that gravel, I shrieked. They were at my house! I screamed so loud that, even though the cameras were still about fifteen feet from my porch, you could hear my scream broadcast on the show. The camera got to my door and I threw it open, still screaming and jumping up and down when they were telling me I'd won. That meant so much to me. I was adamant about not wearing makeup, and so many people had told me I couldn't get on

TV unless I did. I had just proved them all wrong. I was going to be on TV in just two days — and without a stitch of makeup.

My friend Christie had taken time off work to go with me, and we were going to be there for several days after my debut appearance on national television. As usual, I had big plans swirling around in my brain. I had already decided we were going to be at the Oscars, too. It's no fun to dream big alone — I had to bring as many friends as I could to share in the good times!

We went out on the town on Friday night and had a grand old time at the Steve Harvey show. Christie actually got to sing during their audience competition — and even ended up winning. I knew she would win. The next morning we called Chandra, my sister-in-law, to tell her all the fun we were having. She was at work. At the time, she was employed with a prestigious mortgage corporation in our area, and she'd never tested stepping outside of the box in the name of spontaneity if her job could be on the line. That was completely understandable. Her office was very straight-laced and interruptions were not encouraged, but we called anyway. When she answered I said, "Chan, you should have been here last night to hear Christie sing at the Steve Harvey show. She sang like I've never heard her sing before. I was blown away!" Chandra began to whisper, "Wow, that is amazing," and I knew she was at her desk working. I then shared with her that she was invited to join us. I knew she could rarely take off work for anything that was not an emergency, so I didn't press the issue before leaving. But after what Christie had just experienced, I had to call and give Chandra the opportunity to get in on all our fun.

She sadly began to explain how she was at work, and didn't know if she could get time off, or if she could afford a last-minute airline ticket to Los Angeles. But I reminded her, "You have not because you ask not." I told her she needed to ask to take time off, and that the worst they could say is, "No."

"Okay," she whispered, "Let me see what I can do, and I will call you back!" I was surprised — and thrilled — that she was at least going to try. Never let fear or unanswered questions about a situation keep you from experiencing something new. You could be missing out on a moment that could change your life forever. Only thirty minutes or so had passed when Chandra called me back to say that she would be on the earliest flight to Los Angeles. Christie and I were over the moon!

It seemed like only a few minutes had passed before Chandra was beating on our hotel door in Los Angeles. As soon as we finished our celebrating, I quickly began to devise a plan on how we would get to the Oscars. "Wait a minute," Chandra said, "We are going to try to get into the Oscars, too?" She should have known better than to think any trip with me wouldn't involve a little excitement.

Friday morning, I prepared to host the Oscars segment on "Good Day Live" with Arthel Neville, Steve Edwards and Debbie Matenopoulos. It was only supposed to be a 45-second introduction segment, but as the hosts met me and felt my energy, they asked me if I'd ever thought about having my own show. I told them that I'd daydreamed about it off and on, but the idea had never seemed solid. I was wearing my father's praying hands again, and we started to talk about me losing my dad live on the air. Somehow, my 45-second segment turned into 20 minutes on national television. Arthel and Debbie gave me their numbers and addresses and encouraged me to pursue my own show. Again, I looked down at those praying hands and shook my head in amazement.

Now, it was time to get down to the business of the Oscars. Nothing in life goes well without preparation, and I had done my research. I found out they usually block the street off in front of the Kodak Theater at 6 a.m. the day of the awards, and if we were going to be anywhere near that red carpet, we had to be there by then. So, at 4 a.m. on Sunday morning, I shook Christie and Chandra awake to get ready for the Oscars. My plan was to put on our formal attire in the morning, pack our heels and other items into a bag, put on our jackets, hike on over to the Kodak building as early as possible to get the closest spot to the red carpet, and hold that spot until the show started. Mind you, the ceremony doesn't start until 7 p.m., but I wanted to be in the best possible position to see everything we could. We were all yawning as we staked our territory and, as it approached dawn, we could see other people arriving. There were stage managers, famous make-up artists, prop managers, crowd managers, and several others setting up for the Oscars. It was magical to see it all unfold. I'd always known that there had to be tons of people behind the scenes to build the biggest night in Hollywood, but I'd never realized the scope of it. On television, we just see the stars. The people making everything happen are stars, too — we just never hear about them.

Christie and Chandra were getting hungry, and to be quite honest, so was I, but none of us wanted to take a chance on stepping away to look for food. Christie spotted a McDonald's up the block and the three of us debated what to do. As I turned and looked behind me to assess the crowd, I saw there were too many people that would immediately take our front row "seat," so I told the girls that I was fine, I didn't have to eat. I knew they were not going to be okay with standing there 13 hours without anything to eat, so I told them to go and I would make sure no one took their places. I had hardly gotten the words out of my mouth before they took off running. As they got further down the street, I could see they were not immediately able to get into the restaurant. They appeared to be standing around waiting for it to open. I later found out that wasn't the case. We were in downtown Hollywood, after all, and apparently the drunks were already up and getting into trouble. Chandra and Christie found themselves standing right in the middle of a heated drunken argument. Apparently they were able to diffuse the fight by singing praise songs to God. One of the drunken men even sobered up long enough to join them in their singing!

They then returned with breakfast, but I couldn't eat one bite because I was too afraid that I would let my guard down too long and miss an opportunity. The time seemed to fly by as we stood there watching these professionals put together the magic of the Oscars. We were there all day long, and felt a thrill as the red carpet was rolled out. In a way, it seemed like we were in on a secret, like we were seeing a magician reveal his tricks.

As it approached the afternoon, we began to see more and more media stars arrive, such as Star Jones, the hosts of Entertainment Tonight, and Extra. Although they were not the stars that everyone was waiting to see, any familiar face was acceptable at this point since we still had at least ten more hours to go. We killed time by making friends with the people standing around us. We met people from all around the world that day: Russia, England, Venezuela, France, and more. We learned a lot about the people that chose to come out and be a part of this adventure — although we were still the only members of the crowd who were dressed in evening attire! We found ways to entertain ourselves, but the time, along with our aching feet, was starting to get to some of the people that were there. Paranoia set in for a moment and people started to feel like their spots were being jeopardized. This is when tempers began to flare. The crowd that had previously been so friendly was turning hostile, and the next thing we knew, we were standing in the middle of a shoving match that included a very strong and intimidating man, which made us not feel too safe. Christie began to yell out, "Please don't fight!" Chandra had a look of utter confusion, and I was flustered trying to see how I could control this situation. What in the world had I gotten us into?

Thankfully, the scene quickly died down and peace was restored. Several more celebrities from all over the world continued to arrive, and being that we were on the front row, we were interviewed a total of seventeen times! They were interested to know how long we had been standing there and what had possessed us to come out and stand for fourteen hours for this event. I felt inspired and started to conduct my own interviews on the red carpet with the people that were around us. Even when the media would approach us, I'd start to interview them instead. My final interview was with a man named Gary Cogill, who, oddly enough, is from Dallas, too. He agreed with me that Jamie Foxx would win the Oscars, and we then exchanged numbers, as he had to get back to work.

As night began to creep in, the crowd behind us began to get really agitated and pushy. In an attempt to see the celebrities that were arriving, the people in the very back began to press us all on top of one another. There was literally no room, and I felt like we would be crushed by one another. Security suddenly saw all of us as a threat and began to talk about erecting a large fence in front of us to protect the stars that were arriving.

We began to see more and more cars pull up and the celebrities begin to pour in. The sweet, friendly crowd that I was able to control earlier had suddenly turned into an anxious mob! Even so, we saw more stars face to face than we had expected. Kirsten Dunst, Robin Williams, Gwyneth Paltrow, Drew Barrymore, Brad Pitt … and then the one and only Oprah! As these big stars began to approach our area and speak with us, the mob behind just exploded at the chance to touch their hands or speak with them. It was insane. The push and press behind us became so violently scary that I no longer felt safe and decided this adventure was over. Chandra and Christie had already bailed and I was right behind them. As we pressed our way out of there and began to walk back to our hotel room, we could do nothing but shake our heads and laugh about what we had just experienced. We had stood on our feet from sunrise to sundown. We didn't get into the Oscars that night, but we came away with a story of patience, adventure, faith and courage. I'd learned that if we could be open to circumstance, we would see that our plans can sometimes lead us through lessons that are much more rewarding. I thought I wanted to be inside of the Oscars that night, but the real experience was on the outside in the midst of the "no name" stars of this world. I thank God for that experience. I even walked away with a piece of the red carpet someone cut for me.

There are no mistakes or failures, only lessons. -Denis Waitley

Nothing Ventured, Nothing Gained

*"You got a dream... You gotta protect it. People can't do somethin'
themselves, they wanna tell you you can't do it. If you want somethin', go
get it. Period." – Christopher Gardner, "The Pursuit of Happyness"*

At that point, life was good. Artis and I were no longer struggling. We had
a strong marriage, a beautiful house and two amazing children. I was
having one adventure after another, and my faith was growing
exponentially by the day. I should have been completely satisfied with my
life … but there was just one situation weighing on my mind. My mother
had begun dating. I didn't understand how she could be so disloyal to my
dad after thirty years of marriage. I'll admit, I was the opposite of
supportive. In fact, I was downright angry.

As in all love stories, this one had a bit of a twist to it. Before meeting my
dad, Mom had been dating Nathaniel Ewing — and Dad had stolen her
away from him. It was now well over thirty years later, and Nathaniel felt
that he finally had his second chance. As sweet as the story was, though, I
fought that relationship tooth and claw. I pouted about it, complained
about it, and prayed to God that it would end. But yet again, He had other
plans.

Artis and I were getting ready for bed one evening, and as I took stock of
my life, I suddenly thought about my mother, going to bed alone in her
house across the street. I wasn't alone — I had my husband and boys.
How could I begrudge my mother the love and companionship I enjoyed?
She'd been married to my father for thirty years, but he was gone. Would
Dad want her to be alone like this? That's when I finally became honest
with myself: There was no question that my father would want her to be
loved as he'd loved her so long. God had softened my heart, and I realized
I had been wrong.

In September of 2005, we welcomed Nathaniel Ewing into our family with open arms as he and my mom tied the knot. Nathaniel was the happiest man in the world at that moment. "I let her get away once," he beamed, "but she won't get away from me again!" It brought tears to my eyes to see my mother loved again, just as she deserved to be.

Sisters of Savings

To add to our family's joy, my sister, Lynette, added another precious child to the mix. After having her baby, she expressed a desire to stay at home and fully appreciate the joys of motherhood — but, like everyone, it was a question of whether she and her husband could afford to do it. So Lynette began to clip coupons and find ways to use them to their utmost advantage. She learned to seek out grocery stores that double coupons and catalog their ads to take full advantage of combining coupons, sales, and special deals. We soon realized that these techniques could be a viable business in itself by helping others do the same. Our mission was not only to educate families on how to save money on their food bill while increasing the amount of food they could buy, but also to encourage those families to give some of those savings back to charity. Since the international symbol for help is S.O.S., we decided to name our organization Sisters of Savings. Our motto: Smart, Savvy Shoppers ... Spending Less and Giving More.

We created a website and began to give seminars on how to effectively use coupons to cut a family's food budget. We charged for the seminars and gave a portion of the fee back to charity. We also created a shopping buddy program, charging a monthly fee for us to search out and provide our members with the best deals at area grocery stores and coupons emailed to them each week. The response was immediate and amazing. We had people telling us how they were saving 50 to 80 percent on their food bills. Our message to everyone was simple: you'll save so much, you're required to give back.

Our organization and seminars really began to attract attention. We were featured in a newspaper article with testimonials from some of our members. Then, we were invited to do a segment on a local television station. The producers wanted to follow us on a shopping excursion, because what we were doing sounded too good to be true. So, we let the crew follow us while we shopped. During the segment, we brought a $130 grocery bill down to $2 and a $50 bill down to 50 cents — using nothing but coupons and sales.

The word continued to spread, and then, out of the blue, I got an email from Gary Cogill, the Dallas reporter I'd met at the Oscars. He had remembered my "interviews" on the red carpet and thought I'd be perfect for an open position on a local program called "Good Morning Texas." The response to our segments had already captured the interest of Dave Muscari, vice president of product development at WFAA Channel 8, who also produced the "Good Morning Texas" program. Gary introduced me to Dave, who eventually called me in to audition for the show.

I went to audition for the position because, heck, why not? I gave it my best, but unfortunately, they chose someone else. Dave Muscari was impressed, though, with my style and my spark and made it clear that they would be interested in having me on segments in the future. In fact, he wrote me a letter telling me how impressed he was, saying, "nothing ventured, nothing gained." He also said that he saw great things ahead for me and would be proud to be able to say he "knew me when." It was encouraging to hear those words. And he was right: nothing ventured, nothing gained. You have to be willing to take risks to gain anything in life. You have to put yourself out there, take some chances and see what life hands you. If you win, you win. If you lose, you say, "Oh well, I tried." I still have that letter, and read it whenever I become discouraged. Dave was true to his word, and soon offered me a weekly segment on "Good Morning Texas" focused around Sisters of Savings. This was it! I had wanted to be on television for so long, and now the opportunity had presented itself. It was a huge break for Sisters of Savings — and for me. I was ecstatic. I will always think fondly and gratefully of Dave, because he really brought my dreams to reality. Dave allowed me to expand my knowledge and taught me everything I need to know about broadcasting and producing segments. There are people who give and don't know they're doing it. There are people who will mentor you and don't realize what an imprint they are leaving on your life. Dave has given so much to me over the years and not even known it. The show has given me a platform to further my philanthropy. It has handed me opportunities I never could have dreamed of. And it's all thanks to Dave.

Since I was now on television, people recognized me and I was constantly stopped by people telling me how much I helped them and made a difference in their lives. It was so inspiring to see that I was helping people, and I wanted to do more. Helping people is addictive — you can do so much with your life that can help others with theirs. During the course of developing my television segments, I met a reporter who is now a dear friend, named Jeff Crilley, who encouraged me to develop a radio show. I asked him what I needed to do to get it started, and within fifteen minutes I had called five radio stations. I met with the managers to discuss my idea, which was a one-hour show called "The Real Happy Hour." The show focused on interviewing locals and celebrities — everyone from our mayor to George Foreman — about how they were using their lives to make a difference. I signed a contract and I was now truly recognizable, by the general public at least, as a member of the media.

I was trying to make my mark as a journalist and knew I needed a big-name interview to get people's attention. When I heard that Irving "Magic" Johnson was going to be in town for a series of events, I knew that he was exactly the interview I needed. And I was one hundred percent sure that I would get it. The members of my family are all huge Lakers fans, especially my Mom. I, on the other hand, am a Dallas Mavericks fan. That didn't matter, though. I appreciated who Magic was, both on and off the court, and knew I needed to interview him and put that article in the paper. That would get people's attention! I was still learning the ropes as a reporter, but I managed to find out who Johnson's publicist was. I immediately contacted and was given an event schedule. His publicist assured me that if I went to the first event, I'd get the interview I wanted. I showed up at 8 o'clock that morning at St. Phillip's School where Magic was speaking to the students. There were throngs of seasoned reporters from every outlet around Dallas, and as I fell in with the group, they were all looking at me like I didn't belong. *I am supposed to be here, I am supposed to be here*, I kept repeating to myself. But as Magic finished with the kids, he granted interviews with just a few reporters and then moved on. I wasn't one of the ones he spoke with. I was devastated until the publicist announced that Magic would be heading to Roger Staubach's house for a basketball game, and the remaining reporters would get the opportunity to interview him there. So, a caravan of reporters, including me, followed Johnson's motorcade over to Staubach's home, where we all waited patiently while photographers snapped pictures of the game. When the game concluded, the seasoned reporters were each called in to get their interviews. As they got what they needed, I was left behind looking lost and lonely and wondering why I hadn't been called in. His publicist told me there was to be a gala that night, and if I came back, I'd be able to get the interview I so desperately needed.

I went home and got myself all spruced up, put on a fancy dress, and got ready for the gala. I was certain and determined that I would get that interview. Otherwise, I would have felt that the whole day had been wasted. Before you head into something you have to decide for yourself if what you're trying to accomplish is worth the amount of time it might take you to achieve it. Look closely at what you're about to do and determine if the time it may take you would be better spent pursuing another goal. At that point in time, it was worth it to me to pursue Magic Johnson all over the city to get that interview, and hopefully, get his autograph for Mom.

I headed to the gala, and speaker after speaker got up to honor Magic. There were just hordes of people around him at all times, and I was having a hard time finding a way to work my way into the group for my chance to snag even a brief statement, much less a full interview. I kept looking for the opportunity, but just couldn't find the chance. I was getting frustrated and somewhat disgusted with the whole situation. Here it was, 9:30 at night. I had followed this man and his entourage all over town the whole day and I still hadn't gotten my chance to speak with him. I rushed to the elevator, furiously pushed the button to head to the parking area, looked down at the floor and felt the tears begin to well up from frustration. But, all of a sudden, a very large shoe appeared between the closing doors, and when I looked back up, there was Magic Johnson standing right in front of me. "What's wrong?" he asked. "I've been seeing you around here all day long." With eyes full of tears, I told him, "You know, they told me I was going to be able to interview you today, but I haven't been able to do that." He told me, "Well, look. I am staying at the Anatole Hotel. If you come meet me at 9 a.m. tomorrow, I promise I'll give you your interview." I positively floated out of there. I drove home, giggling and bouncing up and down in my seat, excited that what I had set out to do was actually going to happen. When I got home, I told my sons, who were both huge basketball fans, that I had met Magic Johnson and was going to interview him the next morning. They looked at me and said, "Yeah right, Mom." I insisted to them that I really was, but they still didn't believe me.

I got up bright and early the next morning, and as I was getting ready to leave, I asked my boys if they were going to come with me. Neither of them believed I was going to get the interview, so they both declined to come. I said, "Well, give me your basketball then." It was a green and white ball that wasn't even an official NBA basketball, but it was all they had.

The Hilton Anatole Hotel is a luxury hotel in the center of the arts and shopping district of Dallas. It's large and grand just like everything in Texas, and it houses a priceless art collection, multiple bars and restaurants, a private seven-acre park, tennis courts, and so much more. The lobby is lavishly decorated with polished marble floors, cozy yet classy seating areas, and expensive Asian art pieces. It's truly a spectacular site, but nothing looked more spectacular to me that morning than seeing Magic Johnson sitting in the lobby waiting to give me my interview. We talked for a while, and he happily answered all my questions. At the end of our interview, he signed my sons' basketball and signed a picture with a message to my mom. When I triumphantly walked back in the door of our house that day I threw the basketball to my sons, and they couldn't believe I had actually done it.

There are times when you just can't give up, no matter how frustrated you are. Keep your eyes focused on the prize. My prize that weekend for all my hard work and persistence was getting the chance to interview Magic Johnson. I took full advantage of that chance and began to be seen as a serious reporter. Magic has always embodied the idea of giving back. He's active in donating time and money to charitable organizations, especially those involving children. His message is clear: It doesn't matter how much or how little you have — you *always* have something you can give. I don't suppose his "giving" of his time that morning should really be considered charity, but it was definitely the handout I needed to take my career to the next level. Soon after my interview with Magic Johnson, I found out that Will Smith was coming to town for the premiere of his movie, *The Pursuit of Happyness*. I wasn't going to miss a chance to interview him, so I made a point of getting to the red carpet, despite the fact that I didn't have a camera crew. I just had my handheld camera, but was determined to meet Will Smith and get an interview anyway. As I was standing in the line waiting for Will Smith to arrive, there was a gentleman standing next to me who recognized me from "Good Morning Texas." He asked where my camera crew was, and I admitted that I didn't have one. Then, that kind man told me he had two camera guys and could help me record my segment ... for a mere fifty dollars! Fifty dollars? Um, yeah! So, I handed over the money, and he put his additional cameraman with me.

We were situated at the very end of the line of media along the red carpet as Will Smith came out. I was already feeling a bit shunned by the rest of the members of the media because I was the new kid on the block, and as Will made his way down the line of media and it was finally my turn to interview him, someone tapped him on the shoulder and he turned to go. I looked forlornly at one of his security guards, who must have noticed my look of disappointment. So the security guard stopped Will and whispered in his ear, causing him to turn around and look at me. There I stood with my rented cameraman, sadly holding my microphone like a little lost girl waiting for someone to rescue her. Will ran down the red carpet to where I stood, gave me a big kiss on the cheek, and a fantastic interview. He is such a down-to-earth guy and very genuine.

The next time I met him was two years later for the premiere of *Seven Pounds*, and this time I was an official member of the media. He gave me another wonderful interview and, after I finished my interview, I handed the microphone to my son R.J. Will spoke such inspirational words to my son, telling him to be fearless and relentless.

For some reason, my son would later tattoo the word "fearless" across his shoulders.

The Giving Movement and Minnie's Food Pantry

I've learned that people will forget what you said, people will forget what you did, but people will never forget how you made them feel.
– Dr. Maya Angelou

I was finally in the position to pay my bills, feed my family and live a comfortable existence. But maybe part of the problem was just that; I *existed*, but wasn't really living. I was still struggling with what exactly I really wanted to do with my life. I had thought that success would come easily. I'd get married, have kids, stay home to raise my children while my husband supported the family, and help out neighbors and the community when I could. Not exactly what my parents had done, and certainly not ministry, but something similar to how they had led their lives. That had been my idea of success. My views and ideas about success were now changing, evolving if you will. I was born to be a difference maker, to live my life with purpose. I needed something more.

My boys were doing well, my husband's company was successful, and we were all healthy. I really was blessed. It was as if a light bulb suddenly came on, and I realized I had so much to give but wasn't at the time. I was an active member of the church and I was helping my mom with her ministry, but there was still so much more I needed to be doing. I had to do something to honor my mother, Minnie Ewing. Since she had started Helen's House in my grandmother's memory, I had heard my mom say so many times, "I wish my mother could see this." I realized that I never wanted to say those words. I knew that I had to honor my mother now, while she was still with me. After all, my father was gone now and I only had one hero remaining. I was determined to show her how much she meant to me. Have you ever felt that way about someone? Mother was a strong woman. After my dad passed away, she had continued to hold her head up as she carried on her journey alone as the Pastor of DayStar

Deliverance Ministry. So, as a testament to her, I started The Giving Movement.

Humble Beginnings

The Giving Movement was an idea that by giving to one person, it would cause others to continue the chain of giving until it just became widespread. I submitted my application to the IRS to become a 501 (C) (3) charitable organization. This is a fairly lengthy approval process and I was prepared to wait. However, God has a way of nudging things along. Right after I sent my application to the IRS, a massive fire hit an apartment complex in a poor area of Dallas. Children had been displaced, families had lost their homes and belongings, and nobody had anything to eat. As desperate as these people were, it seemed like nobody was willing to help them. I had already been talking to people about what I was planning to do with The Giving Movement, and they began to suggest that I take on that neighborhood and give a voice to those displaced families. I liked the idea and began to think about what I could do to get donations. Then I realized I couldn't legally accept donations on their behalf because I wasn't officially a charitable organization. So I placed a desperate phone call to the IRS. I explained my situation to the woman on the phone and asked if there was any way she could help me — and, by helping me, help these families. She put me on hold for what seemed like an eternity while she went to find my paperwork. When she came back on the line, she told me she had pushed my application through and would fax me the approval so we could immediately accept donations for the victims of the fire. On Valentine's Day, 2007, The Giving Movement was officially born. By trying to help others, I had already spread the spirit of charity when that IRS worker decided to give of her time to dig through stacks of paperwork and approve my application. The Giving Movement was already in motion.

Once I helped the families from the fire, I had to decide how I would focus this new movement. I thought back to the times when I felt most desperate as a young wife and mother, and I remembered all the times we went hungry. I thought about the few items Artis would bring home from his pizza delivery jobs and was reminded how absolutely defeated I felt when I was denied food stamps. That was it. That would be the main strength behind The Giving Movement: I would start a food pantry. It made perfect sense. I would name it after my mom. Minnie's Food Pantry had a nice ring to it. I would honor my mother the same way my mother had been honoring hers. I was thankful that mother would be able to witness my love and admiration for her.

The first thing I needed was office space. Talk about blind faith. I walked into the office complex knowing I would have to sign a lease and having no idea how I was going to pay for it. I knew that I had two months of the lease payment in savings, but I wasn't working, and the money my husband made was tied up in household bills. The more I thought about it, the more I knew my calling was to feed the hungry and help those that were less fortunate than others. So I signed the lease for my space and immediately opened The Giving Boutique.

The premise was that I could sell clothing and accessories, and use that money to purchase food for those in need. Of course, I was just starting out and didn't have much of a following, so just about all the money I made from selling the items in the boutique went toward paying the rent. I quickly began to get frustrated. How was I going to feed people if all the money I made was going into rent? God must have been thinking the same thing because I heard His voice and He told me I was on the wrong path. I wasn't supposed to be running a boutique; I was supposed to be feeding His people.

I placed a call to my realtor and left her a message telling her I was supposed to be feeding the hungry. I also told her God had told me she had a building for me that I needed for my pantry. I didn't hear back from her so I placed a second call and this time she picked up the phone. She said, "So, you need me to get you a location." I said, "Yes." Then she asked, "And, how much do you want to pay per month?" "Nothing," I replied.

"It's supposed to be free." There was a very long silence. She didn't speak and I didn't speak. My mother had taught me that in business, he who speaks first loses. So I remained silent waiting for her response. When she finally spoke, she uttered just one word. "Free? For how long?" she asked. I replied, "Well, my lease is for three years so that's how long I need it to be free." That was the end of the conversation and I had to wait to hear what solution she would provide.

Honestly, I wasn't nervous as I waited for her to call me. I knew this was going to happen on my terms, because God had told me so. I just didn't know what those terms would be yet. "A man's heart plans his way, but the Lord directs his steps."

My realtor walked into my office a few days later and said, "Okay. I have a space for you." I was ecstatic! This was it. I knew I had heard the voice of God. My pantry would finally begin. We walked out of my office and just two doors down. But when I walked into that space, I could hardly believe what I was seeing. There was no ceiling, no flooring, no lights, no electricity … it didn't even have walls. It was a big, empty, run-down space that had nothing. My realtor handed me the keys and said, "I've already priced it. It will cost you $40,000 to build this place out. But, she added, if you pay for the build-out, I'll give it to you for free." I was holding the keys to Minnie's Food Pantry. I would feed the hungry in honor of my mother. And I needed $40,000 to make it come to life. From then on, every time I pulled up to The Giving Boutique, I would look just two doors down at what would eventually be Minnie's Food Pantry. I could hear God telling me every morning, "I told you to feed the hungry." But how in the world was I going to manage that?

There will be times in your life when you hear that quiet voice that tells you to do something. You may not have any idea of exactly how to go about doing it. That is when your faith has to kick in. You have to believe in your purpose. Believe you can achieve it and speak it out loud to yourself. You have to say, "I will do this," and start taking baby steps or one giant step to get it accomplished.

The Makeover

A friend of mine felt I should meet a friend of hers because there would be some great synergy between the two of us. She gave me the woman's number and made me promise I would call her. The number she gave me belonged to Mary Harvey, designer and former wife of comedian Steve Harvey. I wasn't sure what to expect when I called Mary. When I did finally call, I heard a soft-spoken voice and innocent laugh. Mary had an all-around pleasant nature. We talked a few times and Mary asked me if she could come out to see The Giving Boutique. I was struggling to turn my movement into a reality, and since Mary was a designer, I hoped she could give me some ideas on how I should decorate the boutique. Mary came out and I told her all about what I wanted to do. She was full of ideas and suggestions, and I shared my vision with her for The Giving Movement and Minnie's Food Pantry.

A few days later, Mary came back and invited me to her home. It was beautifully decorated from top to bottom, and I could see her impeccable taste everywhere. She led me to her closet, and when she opened it, I saw what had to have been 400 to 500 pairs of shoes. I love shoes, but these were shoes I could never afford to own. Every high-end designer was represented in that closet. Mary asked me what shoe size I wore. When I replied that I wore an eight-and-a-half, she said, "That's what size I wear! Go ahead and pick out a pair." I just stared at her blankly. "I have a feeling you never do anything for yourself," she said. "Go on." When I still just stood there looking at the shoes, Mary took it upon herself to pick out a pair for me. When I put them on, I felt like a kid in a candy store. Mary said, "Pick out another pair." I told her that I would, but for each pair of shoes she gave me I would take a pair from my own closet and put them in the boutique to make money for The Giving Movement. Mary thought that was a wonderful idea and told me, "After you're done picking out the ones you want, I'll box up the rest of the ones I don't need and donate them to the boutique so you can sell them." It was such a generous offer, and I wasn't quite sure how to respond. Mary donated not only several hundred pairs of shoes, but clothes and enough high-end decorative items to decorate the entire boutique. The selling of those shoes alone paid the rent on the boutique for several months. Not only that, but Mary wrote me a check to put towards what I needed to make Minnie's Food Pantry come to life.

I can honestly say Mary did a makeover on both the boutique and my life. Back then, I thought I was doing well to stay away from makeup and jewelry and those kinds of things, feeling as though I was securing my place in heaven by doing so. But lately, I'd started questioning that part of my upbringing. After all, I had never judged other women for wearing makeup. It just began to seem silly to me. So, I did the logical thing and consulted my pastor — my mother. I told her that I was considering giving makeup a try, and asked what the scripture said about it. Surprisingly, my mother was supportive! She even went so far as to announce to our congregation that she saw no reason for women to not wear makeup or pants if they wanted to. It probably sounds strange to most people, but at 37 years old, I couldn't wait to put on my first pair of jeans. The makeup was a little more troublesome, though. I had absolutely no clue how to go about it. Fortunately, Mary stepped in and taught me how to apply my new makeup. As I continued to try to garner donations from very high profile people, I struggled with how to style my modest wardrobe to look more professional. Mary gave me clothing — very expensive clothing. She made over my entire wardrobe and helped me walk with a sense of confidence, no matter whose company I was in. She reaffirmed my belief that people are generous in their nature, but there are those that truly embody that idea. Mary knew how to share a simple smile that could change a person's day, and share of herself to change a person's life.

With the decorative items Mary had given me, the boutique was now decorated much more nicely than our home. That wasn't very difficult to do, mind you. Artis and I had furnished our home by picking up items from the side of the road and near dumpsters on trash days. A good cleaning, and each item became another piece of furniture in our house. It was after redecorating the boutique that I took a good, long look around our home. I had spent so much time trying to give to other people and had put so much effort into helping others build their lives that I hadn't taken the time to fully notice what I had. Our house still had the same furnishings we'd picked up off the side of the road when we first bought the house. I felt sad about that because I truly did appreciate our house, but it didn't really feel like a home. My mom's home was nicely decorated with all the little antiques and decorative items she had collected over the years, and our house looked neglected by comparison. I had told my mom how disheartening it was to come home after working so hard for others and see that I really wasn't providing much for myself. My mom came over one day when I was feeling particularly down about it and asked, "Do you trust me?"

"Of course I do," I answered.

"No," she said. "Do you really trust me?"

What was she getting at? Then my mom said something that made no sense at the time. "If you truly want these things for your home, then you need to give all this away," she said. She meant it, and I trusted her. So I began to give away everything in our home that I wanted new for ourselves. Beds, couches, tables, chairs — everything we had found that I no longer wanted to represent my home went to others who needed it. My husband and boys thought I was crazy. Slowly, our house began to be devoid of most furnishings, and I began to hear the annoyance in the voices of the men in my life as they again questioned my sanity. But I was tired of settling for just good enough. I wanted better and felt I deserved it. At the same time, we barely had anything left in the house and it was affecting my husband and kids. I had already given those items away and had no money to replace them, so I had to trust my mom's wisdom and know that a solution would find its way to me.

Mary Harvey came to visit me in my home one day and, although the house was clean, it was obviously missing some essential items. But she didn't say anything about it. Shortly after that, Mary called me at work and asked me to come to her house yet again. When I got there, she was waiting for me in the foyer. I asked her what was wrong and she said, "Nothing. I've just decided to put this house up for sale." She and her husband had gone through a divorce and Mary decided she had no attachment to anything she owned anymore. "I've got to get everything out of here before this weekend," she continued. So I began to form a plan in my head of how I was going to help her move all this furniture from this massive house and wondered where she was going to store it all. As she handed me the keys to the house, she said something that, yet again, made me just stare at her blankly. "It's yours," she said. When I obviously didn't understand what she was talking about, Mary said, "Everything in this house is yours. I don't need it."

Can you imagine what a gift that was? Mary had not only remodeled my boutique and given me a personal makeover, she was now making over my home. What my mom had said was true. I had given away all my things to those who needed it, and had received replacements in return. Mary's house was much, much bigger than mine and I would never have room for all that furniture. Many of the furnishings, artwork, rugs and electronics Mary gave me that I never in my wildest dreams would have been able to afford to buy for myself, I also in turn gave to others. All in all, Mary helped furnish the homes of five different families that week. She is an incredible woman whose generosity knows no boundary.

What are you willing to sacrifice? Do you want the best for your life or are you willing to just settle? Ask yourself that question each time you take a step in your life. Know what your wants and needs are and express them. You never know what may happen.

Helping Hands
Of course, not everything can be achieved on your own. When I worked for Middlekauff Ford, I had learned how important it was to surround yourself with supportive people who believe in you. My best friend, Erica,

had always been a cornerstone of support for me. She had stood by me through thick and thin. I was struggling to get The Giving Movement and Minnie's Food Pantry off the ground. Erica was doing really well for herself as a customer service manager at a large mortgage firm, with over 400 people who had to answer to her. One day Erica walked into the boutique and said, "I resigned and I have a new job." I was happy for her because I thought, *Boy, someone really must have offered her a lot of money to get her to come work for them.* Erica was brilliant and I knew she'd be an asset to her new employer. I asked her, "Who are you working for?" "You!" she announced proudly. My stomach dropped. Me? I knew I always looked like I had it going on because I carried myself in such a positive manner but, in reality, I had nothing going on, especially in my bank account. The only thing in the bank was H-O-P-E, hope. There certainly wasn't any money and I told my best friend, "Erica, I have nothing to pay you!" She said, "I'm not here for the pay. I'm here to help you because I believe in you." Like I said, it's so important to have those people around you who will push you to the next dimension of reaching your dream. That person for Minnie's and me has been Erica.

With Erica by my side, I began to speak to everyone I would meet about my vision for Minnie's Food Pantry. Not only would I talk about it, I would show them the empty space and tell them what I needed to do to make Minnie's a reality. One day a man named Ray walked into the boutique while I was crying, after a donor who had pledged to give me toys to distribute to needy kids at Christmas had backed out. I had 78 kids expecting to receive gifts and now had no idea how I was going to accomplish that. Ray saw me crying and asked what was wrong so I explained the situation to him. I thought he was just a well-placed shoulder for me to cry on at the moment but he ended up being so much more than that. Ray belonged to an organization that conducted workshops and one of the requisites to passing these workshops was you had to give something back to the community. So Ray "adopted" those 78 children and during the next week began to bring in toys, each wrapped up with a different child's name on it. It was the most incredible thing I had ever seen.

On the last day of that week, a gentleman named Sean came into the office and, as we got to talking, he told me he wanted to start his own non-profit. I shared with him the name of a young lady who could help him and then took him two doors down to show him the space I wanted to turn into Minnie's Food Pantry. Sean listened and looked and smiled. He said, "Wow, you really have big dreams." I did and I knew it. Shortly after that day a lady named Pam called and asked me if I had put my wants and needs for the food pantry into writing. She informed me that another organization may want to help me complete the build out and get Minnie's off the ground. So Erica and I got to work figuring out what we really needed to start the food pantry and what we ultimately wanted to achieve. Within a week we had it all typed up and submitted that information to Pam's organization. Unfortunately, we didn't hear anything from Pam but just the inquiry gave us more hope to deposit into our bank account.

That same week, Sean called me. He asked me if I had been able to complete the renovation and I told him unfortunately, no. Then he asked me, "Well, have you put your needs into writing?" Preparation is so important. If Pam hadn't gotten me to put those requirements into writing, I wouldn't have been prepared to give Sean that information. I told Sean I did have our requirements and he informed me there was an organization that needed to do a project for the community. If I would send him the information he would see if he could get our project selected. Of course I was all prepared and e-mailed it to him right away. The next morning he called me back. "You've been selected!" he exclaimed.

Within a week, 17 workers showed up at my door. I led them to the empty space and they proceeded to install brand new carpet, put up walls, the ceiling, run electrical, and hang lights and everything we needed to prepare the space to become Minnie's Food Pantry. They even brought in and assembled shelves to store the food items. Not only did they complete the work that needed to be done, they did it with excellence and a superb attitude. Every day for seven days they would show up and every day I would cry tears of joy. How symbolic it was that they took seven days to create the food pantry, and it took seven days for God to create heaven and earth. On the seventh day He rested, and on the seventh day, Minnie's was complete. The only thing they couldn't do was run the HVAC system and that was just fine by me. My pantry was done.

I called the health department the next day to set a time for an inspection to get my permit. Artis and I showed up to meet with the health inspector, all dressed up and prepared to celebrate afterwards. The inspector walked through the building, came back to Artis and me and said, "I'm sorry, but there's no way I can approve you." "Why?" I asked in shock. He told us there couldn't be carpeting in an approved food establishment. The risk for bacterial contamination was too great. The look of disappointment on our faces was very obvious at that point. The health inspector said, "Look. If there's no carpet in here while I make my inspection I can give you your occupancy permit right away." We would then have 60 days to get the proper flooring put in to get the food permit, but could occupy the space in the meantime. Artis and I, in our going-out-to-dinner clothes, dropped to our knees and began to tear up that carpet faster than you could say "check, pleas," as the inspector stood there watching us work. It took us two-and-a-half hours to pull up the carpet, but we got that occupancy permit. Now what were we going to do? We had no money to put new flooring down.

The company that conducted the workshops to get Minnie's Food Pantry to this point had given me a certificate to attend the workshop. When I attended the three-day workshop, on the last day, I met a man named Darryl Robertson. Darryl introduced me to his lovely wife, Lisa, and told me he had listened to me talk about the pantry all weekend and wanted to know how he could get involved. I invited him to come and look at the space and told him we were lacking air conditioning. Darryl was a builder and committed to donating an air conditioning unit to the pantry that day. I couldn't believe what a generous gesture that was. So when we had to pull the flooring up, I remembered Darryl and called to see if he could help us out. He asked what we needed and I told him we needed floor tile because we had to pull the carpet up. Otherwise, we wouldn't get our food permit and there would be no pantry. Darryl made some calls and gave me the address of a company to go see who had agreed to donate the tile we needed. Erica and I headed over immediately and, when we got there, saw the tile was a rainbow of colors. But, free is free and we were excited to finally have everything we needed to open the doors to Minnie's. As we were loading up the tile the gentleman who was helping us asked, "Do you know how to install tile?" Neither one of us did. "Do you have the mastic and grout to put in the tile?" We just looked at each other blankly. Again, the answer was no. Erica and I joke that cameras should be on us everywhere we go because it's definitely a God thing — He's always opening doors for us.

As we walked into the showroom I approached the young lady at the counter and told her I was from the food pantry. She said they had been expecting me and I began to tell her the story of what had happened with the flooring. I had passed a man on my way in who was sitting and talking on his cell phone. He suddenly hung up the phone and interjected himself into the conversation. "Do you know how to lay down tile?" he asked. I gave him the same answer, no. He said, "Okay, you convinced me."
"I did?" I asked. "Convinced you of what?"
He said, "I'll put the tile down."
"Who are you?" I asked in shock.
"I own this place," he said. "And this will be my good deed for the day."
He asked how soon we needed the tile installed and I said, meekly, "Um, tomorrow morning?"
Mind you, this was a Friday afternoon, but he agreed. Then I said, "I have to warn you, the tile is not all the same color."
And his response was just as biblical as the entire process had been. He said, "Well, didn't Joseph have a coat of many colors?"
"Yes, sir!" I replied.

"Well, then," he replied. "I guess Cheryl will have a floor of many colors." As promised, his crew showed up bright and early Saturday morning to install the tile.

Once again, angels had been sent our way and the pantry was finally a reality. It wasn't easy, but we got what we needed and it's continued that way to this day. There have been more times than I can count when we needed something for Minnie's and someone, somehow, has stepped in to help. Just one example was when I was visiting Terri Tanner, the owner of a local bookstore. She and I were talking and as I got ready to leave she said, "Cheryl, we used to have a café here and I put some boxes of items in your car that I'd like to donate to the pantry." I thanked her for her generosity and headed back to Minnie's. As I listened to my voicemails along the way, there was a message from Erica in a panic, saying we had no breakfast items to give out to the people and no funds to go buy any. When I got to the pantry, we unloaded the boxes while talking about what solutions we could come up with to provide breakfast foods. But as we opened those boxes, what did we find? It was cereal — boxes and boxes of cereal. That story has happened over and over again in some form or another. Each time, God has provided exactly what we needed.

It may come as a surprise to some, but the most difficult hurdle to creating The Giving Movement and Minnie's Food Pantry was my mother. Up until I launched my ministries, I had been working with my mother on The Touch Ministry, which she had founded to honor her mother and my grandmother, Helen Allen. The purpose of Minnie's was to honor my own mother while she was still with me, but Mom still couldn't understand why I would leave The Touch Ministry. It was a very difficult transition for both of us. Fortunately, though, we received some help in that area from Dr. Maya Angelou.

My mother has always been a huge fan of Dr. Maya Angelou, and so have I. While my mother and I were in disagreement, I learned that Dr. Angelou had requested to hear from people whose grandmothers had impacted their lives with strong family values. So, I wrote a letter about my grandmother, and was chosen to be one of those she would interview on her radio show. On October 8, 2008, Dr. Angelou interviewed me, and I got the chance to talk all about Mrs. Helen Allen and how she had impacted my mother and me. I recalled how she made giving the fabric of our lives. I cried as I recalled the woman Mrs. Helen Allen was and the person she helped me become. Then, I transitioned into how my mother, Minnie Ewing, had impacted my life. I was talking to America's Grandmother about my mother and my grandmother. It was a very fitting way for my mom and I to move from one chapter of our relationship to another. And, henceforth, the world knew my mother's name. Finally, after much prayer, my mother said she understood why starting The Giving Movement and Minnie's Food Pantry was so important to me. It was a huge relief and a burden lifted.

God Provides

Never think you need to apologize for asking someone to give to a worthy cause, any more than as though you were giving him or her an opportunity to participate in a high-grade investment. The duty of giving is as much his or hers as is the duty of asking yours. – John D. Rockefeller, Jr.

This is what I was destined to do. I have dedicated my life over the last several years to feeding the hungry and providing for underprivileged children, and I've used my media outlets to help me do so. Every step along the way, we've encountered angels. Erica and I have sat in our office countless times wondering how we were going to pay the light bill or fill the shelves. And countless times someone has intervened and answered our prayers. I am a firm believer that if you are doing what you were called and destined to do, God will help you through. He will not set you on a path, your true path, unless He is willing to hold your hand along the way and carry you when necessary.

2009 was a hard year for all of us. With a failing economy we saw more and more people coming into the pantry needing food. It was a struggle to keep up with the overwhelming needs of so many families. I know that God has put his stamp of approval on our pantry because every month the bills came due, there was someone who would write a check to pay them. During one particularly tight month, a woman brought a friend to the pantry. That woman was so impressed with how we treated her friend that she came back later and paid our bills for two months. I am constantly amazed at people and their generosity. Time and time again, we managed to fill our shelves and give to those who needed it the most.

Not only do we provide food throughout the year for those in need, we also give Christmas presents to children who otherwise wouldn't have anything. And as 2009 drew to a close and we approached the Christmas season, our phones rang off the hook daily with calls from people asking to add their children to the list. That year, we ended up with more than 200 children who needed a toy for Christmas. It was absolutely overwhelming and heartbreaking at the same time. I knew we couldn't let these families down, but had no idea how we were going to raise enough donations to get these kids their gifts and enough money to feed all these families. When we broke down the budget, the final number was staggering. We had to raise $10,000 to get us through the season just in food for Christmas alone. That's a phenomenal amount of money, even in good times. Add the bad economy and unemployment rate to that and it seemed an insurmountable task. As usual, Erica and I set to it.

I placed more phone calls that season than I have in my entire life. I spent hours upon hours calling and begging people to donate. Even our usual benefactors were struggling themselves and couldn't donate what they normally would. One person who did come through for us was Major League Baseball player Torii Hunter of the Los Angeles Angels and his wife, Katrina.

I met with Torii and Katrina and shared with them my goals and visions for feeding the hungry and providing for children in need. As we talked, Torii shared with me his upbringing, remembering standing in food lines with his grandmother. He had grown up in a rough area in Pine Bluff, Arkansas, where most of the kids in the area didn't graduate from high school. In fact, the neighborhood had one of the highest crime rates in the U.S. He remembered sitting around the house playing cards by candlelight because they couldn't pay the electric bill. His mother was the strength of the family, working as a teacher and managing to have all four of her boys in Little League — and attending all of their games.

As we swapped stories of our personal struggles, our hearts and minds connected. He and Katrina vowed to help us, and wrote me a check for $2,500.00 for the pantry. It was a far cry from our goal but was the only large monetary donation I had received all season. I was extremely grateful. Then Torii told me if I didn't manage to raise the rest of the money we needed, to call him and he and Katrina would make up the difference. I was flabbergasted at their kindness but hoped I wouldn't have to make that call.

I continued to make my phone calls to get donations — while the phone calls continued to come in asking for our help. It was overwhelming. I kept thinking, *God, I know you called me to do this but this is such a burden for one person to take on their shoulders!* I walked miles upon miles knocking on doors, lost my voice making phone calls, and still couldn't scrape together enough. The economy made it impossible to accomplish our goals. I finally had to break down and make that phone call to Torii and Katrina. They were true to their word. When I told them the position we were, in they told me to come on over and pick up the check. Torii and Katrina donated $10,000 that we earmarked for the holiday distributions. I will never forget their generosity.

We were absolutely, finally, prepared for all those kids to have a wonderful Christmas. We arranged for the families to come pick up their gifts the week before the holiday, so the kids could have something waiting for them on Christmas morning. The looks on the parents' faces as we handed out video game consoles, bikes, DVD players and all kinds of wrapped gifts for the children was well worth my sore throat and the blisters on my feet. Our entire parking lot was filled with food, thanks to the money Torii and Katrina had donated, and we gave each family the fixings for their Christmas dinner. My mom, Minnie, was out there with us giving away toys and bikes and free hugs. The kids cried because they got a toy; the parents cried because they were so appreciative; I cried because they were all so touched. It was the biggest giving event we've ever had at the pantry, and it was like heaven on earth for me. I knew every time I looked into someone's eyes that day that I was serving my purpose in this world.

The big giveaway happened on December 19th, but we still had plenty to do. People were coming in the week of Christmas, telling us we were their only source of food. We were handing out double amounts, because we planned to be closed from Christmas to New Year's to give our volunteers a well-deserved break. We had enough food in the warehouse to get us through the start of the year while we made calls to get more food donations, so now we could enjoy time with our loved ones, comfortable in the knowledge that we would be able to serve those in need after the holidays. But, yet again, God had different plans.

At the beginning of this book, I told the story of Christmas Eve, 2009. The winter storm had practically shut down the city. Church services and community events were being cancelled, and many families had to cancel their Christmas Eve celebrations because the roads were so slick and dangerous. It was in these conditions that one of our volunteers drove back to the pantry to pick up a last-minute donation. She arrived to find the collapsed roof, the flooded storage area, and the hundreds of pounds of destroyed food. It was a devastating blow.

But, I also told the story of how the community jumped into action. People came together like I'd never before seen, and I was shocked as angel after angel called to ask what they could do to help. At one point, a man named Moses came to the pantry and we spoke as he walked through the destruction. As he left, he asked me, "Why do you feed the hungry?" I was a little surprised by his question, but gave the only answer I could. "I was born to do this," I said. Moses smiled and said, "I'll see what I can do," as he walked to his car.

Looking back, everything was so biblical. Remember, it was my husband, Artis, who years earlier had donated $10,000 to our church when the roof collapsed. Who knew we would sit years later in the same scenario? And how amazing was it that a man named Moses would send us a check for $10,000? Soon after, a high-profile celebrity called our office and donated another $10,000. It was all a miracle — Artis' gift had come back to us twofold.

My team came back together with their sleeves rolled up, and they didn't mind working over the holidays. Shelves were being put back up. Donations were coming in. And, although we didn't have the surplus we'd had originally, I was thankful we would at least have something to give at the start of the year. I was also thankful for that last-minute Christmas Eve donation — because if it hadn't been for that donation, we wouldn't have known about the flooding for another week and the damage would have been much, much worse.

Earlier that month, I'd met the governor of Texas, Rick Perry. I was truly honored as people told him of the many hats I wore, but I was most proud to be able to tell Governor Perry about Minnie's Food Pantry. I told him that I was going to end hunger in the state of Texas and that I would share my blueprint with others. Governor Perry then said something that both surprised and confused me. He said, "Cheryl, I am going to choose Minnie's Food Pantry as the recipient of a friendly wager." I had no idea what he meant at the time, but four days after the Christmas Eve catastrophe, I received the following press release:

> *AUSTIN – Gov. Rick Perry today placed a friendly wager with Georgia Gov. Sonny Perdue over the outcome of today's Independence Bowl game between the Texas A&M University Aggies and the University of Georgia Bulldogs.*
>
> *"Georgia has a tremendous football program, but they're going to find out the hard way just why Texas is the center of the football universe," Gov. Perry said. "As an Aggie myself, you might say I'm biased, but I've seen this team grow each week under Coach Sherman, and I know the Aggies will take home a victory and send the Bulldogs back home to Georgia."*
>
> *In the spirit of friendly competition, Gov. Perry has wagered Mesquite Smoked Peppered Beef Tenderloin*

donated by the Perini Ranch Steakhouse in Buffalo Gap. When the Aggies beat the Bulldogs, Gov. Perry will donate the food from Georgia to Minnie's Food Pantry in Plano.

Can you imagine my surprise? I can't explain the emotions that I had. In the midst of all of my devastation, a ray of hope was shining through. I am a living witness that dreams can come true, and that if you stay persistent, there is no limit to what can happen in your life.

The Perfect 10

Well done, is better than Well said – Benjamin Franklin

May 10, 2010, was a culmination of 10. It was 10 years of *O Magazine*, 10 different charities that would benefit from the event and 10 encounters I've had with Oprah Winfrey over the years. And what a culmination it was!

Oprah was hosting her "Live Your Best Life Weekend" in New York, celebrating her magazine's 10th anniversary with workshops, a charity walk and a myriad of other events. I had been counting down the days. I had selected a participating charity to walk for, No Kid Hungry, and had begun to raise money for the event online. I bought my tickets, made my plans and prepared to give Oprah a few chapters of this very book. She has been such an inspiration, and I wanted her to see how she had impacted my life and the lives of others.

We arrived in New York City on a Wednesday morning and began our magical weekend at "The Dr. Oz Show." We were thrilled just to be going, but when we were seated in the second row, we couldn't believe our luck! Before the show, an announcement was made that a seat number would be called, and the person sitting in that seat would get to be Dr. Oz's assistant for the day. As the room continued to fill up, they repeatedly made that announcement — and each time, I would say, "It's going to be number 17! It's going to be me!" I said it over and over again. I spoke it out loud for everyone to hear. When the show finally started, Dr. Oz began to speak about easy changes you can make in your life to improve the health of your brain. Listening to him talk about Alzheimer's disease was sobering, but it also inspired me to live a healthier life, and to insist the same for my loved ones.

The point arrived when it was time for Dr. Oz to choose a number. And, just as I had known, he chose none other than number 17! I screamed and leaped onto the stage, giving Dr. Oz a big Texas-sized hug as I giggled and jumped up and down. He handed me the coveted lab coat and assisted me in putting on my new gear. Dr. Oz then proceeded to educate the audience about the different things that can be done to prevent Alzheimer's disease. First, he had a bag with items that would help prevent the disease, and I had the audience help me guess what they were (greens, berries, fish and nuts). Next, he had me put on the gloves, which usually means something messy is coming, then led me to a table with a cloth cover on it, which is also not generally a "good" sign. Sure enough, he lifted the cover off to reveal ... human brains. Gross! For a split second, I had second thoughts about being his assistant, but I pushed on the brains just as he instructed me, and described the sensation for the audience. Not only did I survive holding those brains, it wasn't that bad at all! I was Dr. Oz's assistant for the day and that's all that mattered to me. After the show, he even allowed Erica and me to come backstage for an official meet and greet. It was the beginning of what would turn out to be an amazing weekend, and it all happened because I said it would!

That evening we had tickets to the play *Fences* with Denzel Washington, and when we got to the theater, I noticed comedian and radio host, Steve Harvey, having a conversation with Denzel's wife, Pauletta. Of course, I knew Steve (he had been married to my good friend and guardian angel, Mary Harvey), so I stopped by to say hello. Steve introduced me to Pauletta, and when he excused himself to find his seat, Pauletta and I continued our conversation. Apparently, the folks working the house saw us speaking and assumed Pauletta and I were good friends. So they took me up to meet the house manager, Joe. He was very nice, and he gave me his card, telling me that if I needed anything to just give him a call. Something told me I would be calling Joe sometime in the near future.

On Friday, Oprah hosted her show from Radio City Music Hall. Erica and I weren't at the show, but we talked about seeing Oprah another way. Was it possible for Denzel to be in a play and Oprah being in town and not go to see it? We didn't think so. So we called around trying to get another pair of tickets for *Fences*. We searched the Internet, we called friends, we called strangers. There was absolutely nothing available. The play started at eight o'clock and by seven we still hadn't come up with tickets. I decided it was time for Plan B. I picked up my purse, emptied it on the bed, and searched frantically for Joe's card. When I held it up triumphantly, Erica and I just laughed. We knew what was about to happen. I called him and put the phone on speaker so Erica could hear. It rang four times and went to voice mail. How anticlimactic! But I remained confident that we would hear back in time. Sure enough, Joe returned my call. He said he couldn't promise anything, but to be at the theater at 7:45 sharp. Erica and I were dancing as we got dressed to the nines.

We arrived promptly at 7:45, just as Joe had instructed us to do, and there was a huge crowd of people jostling to get tickets. But when we asked one of the staff for Joe, he immediately met us at the box office with two beautiful tickets. I asked him where we would be seated, and he just grinned and said mysteriously, "I think you'll be pleased." So we entered the theater and discovered that we were seated in the eighth row — and seated a mere four seats exactly in front of us were Gayle King and the one-and-only Ms. Oprah Winfrey! "Pleased" was an understatement! Erica and I just looked at each other in amazement. The theater only sat about 1,000 people, and of course everyone had noticed Oprah. Cameras were flashing, and the ladies were very cordial, but I knew they had come to enjoy the play and I chose not to approach her at that moment. I knew, though that this would be the night where preparation would meet opportunity. This would be my tenth encounter with Oprah, and I was determined to make it the perfect ten. What I didn't know yet was how.

At intermission time, everyone in the seats between Oprah and me got up and headed to the lobby. It was like the parting of the seas. I watched Oprah as she turned to say something to Gayle, but then she caught sight of me out of the corner of her eye. Oprah just looked at me and smiled, as if to say, *It's okay. You can talk to me*. I took that opportunity and moved closer to her. Oprah and I began to talk and I reminded her that she had given me my first interview. She said she remembered. I told her she was at the play with her best friend and so was I. She smiled even more. I thanked her for her thoughtful letter she had written to me after she read my article and told her what an impact she had made on my life. I told her, "This is full circle. You talked to me seven years ago about living my dreams and passions. You challenged me to do that." I continued by telling her I had written a book about my experiences and that I would love for her to read it. "I would love to read it," she said. "Give it to me, and I promise I will read it."

My eyes welled up with tears. This was a moment I had waited for. Things truly had come full circle. This was a way of saying "thank you" to her for inspiring me to follow my dreams. It was validation of everything I had done for the last ten years and that I was following my destiny. I gave her the chapters I had printed and we settled back to enjoy the rest of the play. I floated out of that theater that night. Erica and I could hardly believe what had just happened. I had said it would happen and I had spoken it into reality. I knew I would get the chance to give Oprah the chapters, and I did. "Oprah has your book." Every few minutes, Erica would look at me, giggle, and say, "Oprah has your book." I thanked God for what he had done for me. My journal read:

Friday, May 7, at 9:10 p.m., I gave Oprah Winfrey a copy of my book. I am in bed now and I hope I can go to sleep. Tomorrow will be another huge day, I can feel it.

Saturday morning came quickly. It was the official start to the "Live Your Best Life Weekend," and we had chosen to participate in both Dr. Oz's workshop and Nate Berkus' workshop. There were 6,000 people at this workshop and three different seminars happening at the same time. It was insane, and somehow Erica and I got separated. I was upstairs and she had already headed downstairs to grab our seats for Dr. Oz. As I went to head down to find Erica I glanced over and recognized a fantastic woman named Cathie Black. Ms. Black is the president of Hearst Magazines and has been called "The First Lady of American Magazines." She manages the financial performance and development of 14 publications.

It had been only two weeks ago that I'd tried to win an auction to have lunch with Cathie Black in anticipation of publishing this book. Unfortunately, my travels to New York made me miss the ending of the auction, so I could not continue to bid. Imagine my excitement at seeing this publishing icon standing just a few feet from me just the morning after being able to hand Oprah chapters of this very book. The scene was chaotic and Cathie was standing with five gorgeous ladies in her entourage trying to get downstairs. Everyone was being told there was no additional space to go downstairs, that it was full. Of course, Cathie has an all access pass, so they moved back and allowed Cathie and three of the women with her to go downstairs. For some reason, though, they blocked the remaining two women. Those two women seemed to be very soft-spoken. They tried to tell the security woman blocking their way that they were with Cathie, but they couldn't get their point across. Their merits alone could have granted them access. Those women were with a very influential industry mogul and they were supposed to be with Cathie downstairs. So, I intervened. I approached the security woman blocking the escalator and I asked, "Do you know who they're with? They are with Cathie Black. If you don't let them go down, I'm going to have to ask for your name and inform whoever's in charge that you did not let members of Cathie's party go downstairs with her." I looked challengingly at the security guard, who was beginning to look a little nervous about the situation. She certainly didn't know who I was and I'm not sure if she knew who Cathie Black was, but I'm certain that what I said had scared her. After looking at Cathie's friends, back to me, and back to them a few times, the security guard finally moved back from the escalators and said, "Those two can go, but you can't." Like that was going to happen. "No," I said. "I'm going, too." And I walked downstairs and never looked back.

The other hundreds of women standing around the escalators trying to get downstairs just stared as I strolled right past the security guard and headed downstairs with the ladies from Cathie Black's party. Hey, I was supposed to be there, too. When I got downstairs, I searched all over and finally found Erica. "Erica, look, there's Cathie Black!" I said excitedly. I'm sure Erica had no idea who Cathie was either, but she nodded and smiled. She knows that if I'm interested in a person, they must be important. I walked over to Cathie and introduced myself and told her I had attempted to win lunch with her. She was very warm and pleasant. But then I told her I had a question for her. "What are you doing here, out here with us?" I asked. This was Cathie Black and here she was mixed with all these regular women who were standing around waiting to enter. "Honestly," she said, "I'm supposed to be in there already, but I don't even know where to go right now." So I told her, "I don't know the answer to that but I will get the answer." I walked over the girl holding the doors and I said, "Excuse me, that's Cathie Black over there and she's not supposed to be out here. She's supposed to be in there." The lady responded by saying, "Well, I'm sure Cathie knows where she's supposed to go." I told her obviously she didn't or I wouldn't be over here getting the answers for her! Thankfully, the girl got on the radio to find out where Cathie was supposed to be. In the meantime, I went back to Cathie and we began to chat a bit while she was waiting. At the same time, the two ladies in Cathie's party whom I had helped get downstairs were relaying the story to her with much appreciation.

When the young lady approached with her radio, she apologized to Cathie and told her she would be escorted inside to get her seats. As they were escorting her away, Cathie turned to me and said, "Cheryl, c'mon with us." There I was, a plain ol' girl from Dallas, Texas, being escorted in with Cathie Black's entourage! And as we were walking, several other people who were standing around waiting to go in were wondering who we were and why were we going in. I thought to myself, *I'm supposed to be inside now, that's why*, and I smiled as I walked past the crowd.

Erica and I went in with the group and were seated in the front row. Cathie and the rest of her party chose the second and third rows; I'm sure they are used to being at events like this so it was no big deal to them. We really had a chance to sit and talk with her at that point and pick the brain of this media mogul. It was amazing. And, of course, we were all there to see Dr. Oz, and I was excited to be there. I was singing and dancing and getting people up out of their seats to dance with me. You have to enjoy these experiences, after all. About fifteen minutes before the start of the program, a stagehand came out and put an extra chair next to where we were sitting and said it was for someone special. I had no idea who it could possibly be but it sounded exciting. And who comes around the corner to take that seat; Dr. Oz's beautiful wife, Lisa. Lisa Oz would be sitting right next to me for the entire workshop! People kept coming up before the program started to thank her for everything she had done for them. She was kind and genuine and seemed to be a wonderful person.

We introduced ourselves to her as Erica and Cheryl, and she asked us where we were from. "Dallas," I replied.

She immediately asked, "Are you Cheryl *Jackson* from Dallas?" Huh? Did she just ask me that question? How on earth did she know my last name? When I told her yes, that's who I was, she said, "My husband has just been talking about you! He told me about the great time he had with you on his show." I almost fell out of my chair.

The program started, and about fifteen minutes into the seminar, Dr. Oz was talking about the easy changes we can make to our lives to be healthier. He was sharing a wealth of knowledge, and then he stopped and asked, "Where is Cheryl?" My heart almost leaped right out of my chest. I jumped up out of my seat and shouted, "That's me, and I'm here, right where I was supposed to be!" I was escorted to the side of the stage, and as I waited to be brought up, I started crying. So many moments had already happened during those few days, and here was yet another amazing experience. Dr. Oz finally called me on the stage and continued to talk about healthy lifestyle choices. He measured my waist and asked me my height and, to my pleasant surprise, told me my waist size is perfect for my height. It was another surreal experience to have this sweet, accomplished man pull me from a crowd of thousands to come assist him again.

We were scheduled to go to Nate Berkus' seminar next, and that's where Erica and I headed. We were seated in the second row and Nate began to talk about his design theories. One of the things he said was, "As you're decorating your rooms, you should always include photos of beautiful moments." He happened to make eye contact with me just then and I said, "Like this one we're sharing right now?" Nate thought that was great, and he said, "You are now my friend. And I'm going to talk to my friend and make sure my friend is happy." So throughout his workshop, Nate would come by me and ask, "Are you happy? Are you happy with what I'm saying?" Everyone would laugh and he would continue with what he was saying. It was an absolute blast. The next day, Erica and I walked for the charity we had picked: No Kid Hungry. The walk reminded me of my experience by the red carpet at the Oscars — the world is full of so many "no name" stars. I cherish every chance I get to meet these unsung heroes. The entire weekend was amazing. But, more than being just fun, everything that I knew to be true for my life was validated through these powerful men and women who had achieved success for their own lives. I had known where I was supposed to be before, but now I'm surer than ever. I know where I'm supposed to be and who I'm supposed to be, and I am walking into my destiny.

Remember that list of goals I wrote down years ago?

> **Be a better wife and mother.** Always. This is a goal that is never truly completed, and I will continue to strive for that ideal every day for the rest of my life.
>
> **Have my own newspaper column.** Yes. I had gone from delivering newspapers to writing for newspapers — first for *Minority Opportunity News*, and eventually for *The Dallas Morning News*.
>
> **Interview Oprah and be on the Oprah show.** Yes. I got my interview, and went on to meet Oprah nine more times — a "Perfect 10."

Meet Denzel Washington. Yes. I met Denzel and his lovely wife, Pauletta, at the "Live Your Best Life Weekend" in New York.

Host my own radio show. Yes. I hosted "The Real Happy Hour" and interviewed givers about how they were using their lives to make a difference.

Host my own television show. No. Or, as my parents taught me when I was a child, just add a "t" to the end and turn it into "not yet."

What are you passionate about?
Do it right now, Do it right now, Do it right now.

-Cheryl "Action" Jackson

There are good ideas and there are God ideas. Giving is both.
– Pastor Minnie Hawthorne-Ewing

Epilogue: Passing It On

It only takes a spark to get a fire going, and soon all those around can warm up in its glowing. That's how it is with God's love; once you've experienced it, you spread the love to everyone. You want to pass it on.
– Kurt Kaiser, "Pass It On"

Artis and I beat the odds. We married too young and fought poverty for years, but we made it work through faith and persistence. It has been almost 25 years since we married, and I am so blessed to have him and our two sons. I will say to parents who don't think their children are watching them: 90 percent of everything I do and believe was taught to me by one generation or another. Whether it was taught directly to me by my mother, or through her by my grandmother, it was something I learned from my parents.

I learned that giving to others is the only form of receiving. If you do for others, things will be done for you. I learned that you have not because you ask not. If at first you are told "No," just add a "t" to the end and turn it into "Not yet." I learned that hard work pays off. I learned that whatever you want from God, if you really have faith and you believe it, then you claim it. I learned that every life brought into this world has a purpose, and I learned to never stop learning.

Now, I pass on these lessons and more to my two sons. Make sure your loved ones take their health seriously. Make room in your life for what you need; if you want new things, first give away the old. You can choose to fail, or you can choose to take the little opportunities presented to you and use them. Never forget where you came from and the people who helped you along the way. Only one person needs to believe that you will succeed — and that person is you.

I look at my sons today and see our family's fourth generation of givers coming into their own. My younger son, Artis, Jr., works with his father. He is enjoying all the facets of running a company and writing proposals for new clients, and he says that he wants to take over his father's business one day. During the week, Artis, Jr., helps me load and unload food at Minnie's when I need him. He has a Christmas spirit all year long, and a smile that can brighten anyone's day. My eldest son, R.J., is a musician and producer. He is taking on more and more responsibility at Minnie's Food Pantry as we expand our hours, and he will be the person operating the pantry in the evenings. I am always thrilled when he joins to at my speaking engagements. Someday, I know I will watch my sons teach their children — my grandchildren — to live and give in faith.

I often recite the *Prayer of Jabez*. It is a prayer asking God to bless us with the spiritual gifts that allow us to reach the entire world — our "territory" — with His love.

> *Jabez cried out to the God of Israel, "Oh, that you would bless me and enlarge my territory! Let your hand be with me, and keep me from harm so that I will be free from pain." And God granted his request. – 1 Chronicles 4:10*

My prayer for the world is that giving becomes more than a movement. In my family, it's a heritage, a way of life passed on from generation to generation. For us, it isn't about paying it back or paying it forward — nobody needs a reason to give time or money or even a simple hug to someone in need. Imagine what the world would become if all parents passed on to their children this one truth: Give what you have, and God will provide.

Join The Giving Movement

The story doesn't end here. To arrange for Cheryl Jackson to speak at your conference or event go www.cherylactionjackson.com. To receive her weekly "Take Action" e-newsletter challenge please register on the website. Share your thoughts with Cheryl at cactionjackson@me.com.